Orientalism

VISIONS OF THE EAST IN
WESTERN DRESS

Christmas 1994

Orientalism

VISIONS OF THE EAST IN WESTERN DRESS

Richard Martin and Harold Koda

THE METROPOLITAN MUSEUM OF ART

Distributed by Harry N. Abrams, Inc., New York

This volume has been published in conjunction with the exhibition
"Orientalism: Visions of the East in Western Dress," held at The Metropolitan Museum of Art
from December 8, 1994, through March 19, 1995.

Published by The Metropolitan Museum of Art, New York

Copyright © 1994 by The Metropolitan Museum of Art, New York

John P. O'Neill, Editor in Chief

Barbara Cavaliere, Editor

Bruce Campbell, Designer

Matthew Pimm, Production Manager

Library of Congress Cataloging-in-Publication Data

Martin, Richard (Richard Harrison)

Orientalism: Visions of the East in Western Dress / by Richard Martin and Harold Koda.

96 p. cm.

ISBN 0-87099-733-5 (pbk.)—ISBN 0-8109-6490-2 (Abrams)

1. Costume—United States—History—19th Century—Exhibitions. 2. Exoticism in art—United States—
History—19th Century—Exhibitions. 3. Costume—Africa—History—19th Century—Exhibitions. 4.
Costume—Asia—History—19th Century—Exhibitions. 5. Costume Institute (New York, N. Y.)—
Exhibitions. I. Koda, Harold. II. Title.

GT610.M18 1994

390'.09182'1—dc20   94-23522

CIP

The color photographs of apparel in this volume are by Karin Willis, The Photograph Studio,
The Metropolitan Museum of Art

Printed by Meridian Printing Company, East Greenwich, Rhode Island

Cover: Left: Jean Paul Gaultier. Tartar coat ensemble, 1994. Orange brocaded satin and pale blue fake-fur
coat with multicolored Lycra bodysuit and satin pants. Courtesy Jean Paul Gaultier. Right: Jean Paul
Gaultier. Tartar pants ensemble, 1994. Red and gray quilted satin jacket with pale blue angora sweater, green
crinkle-crepe overdress, and fur-trimmed chartreuse satin brocade pants. Courtesy Jean Paul Gaultier.

Frontispiece: Thea Porter. Caftan, ca. 1969. Printed silk. Courtesy Eleanor Lambert.

Note: Unless otherwise indicated, the costumes illustrated in this publication are in the collection of
The Costume Institute, The Metropolitan Museum of Art.

Contents

Foreword

Orientalism, the historical term used to describe the West's fascination with and assimilation of the ideas and styles of the East, is richly represented in the collections of the Metropolitan, specifically in the areas of European and American paintings, sculptures, and decorative arts. The Costume Institute's collection of dress is unrivaled in its holdings of Western Orientalist costumes, and this exotic cache has inspired Richard Martin, Curator, and Harold Koda, Associate Curator, to organize this book and the exhibition that accompanies it.

The project continues the authors' ongoing efforts to explore and display the Museum's grand historical collection of costumes. Their purpose is to use that goldmine of material to define the resonances of the past that reside in contemporary design and to discover and convey the relationships that occur between historical and contemporary cultural issues through fashion. *Orientalism: Visions of the East in Western Dress* is therefore based on both examples from The Costume Institute and loans that include the most recent work of important contemporary designers. The earliest costume, a 1906 gift to the Museum from J. Pierpont Morgan, is a Portuguese man's cape made from late-seventeenth-century Ming Dynasty velvet. The latest two are loans from designers: a Chinese-inspired ensemble by Jean Paul Gaultier and a North-African-influenced gown by Giorgio Armani, both created in 1994. The result of this fertile mix is a dazzling array of luxurious fashions that portrays the enthralling and significant history of Orientalism that has unfolded over the past three centuries.

Philippe de Montebello
Director, The Metropolitan Museum of Art

Introduction

Orientalism is a fabrication of the West. The perilous voyages to Cathay and Edo, and even the narrower crossing to the mysterious harems and itinerant lifestyles of North Africa and the Middle East, gave Europe a secular heaven-on-earth, a paradise undefiled by Western civilization. To be sure, vessels sailed under flags of faith, commerce, and nation, but the voyagers sought more than conversion and other than chattel or geographical attenuation. The early discoverers and the traders sought a land never to inhabit, ever to see as different—a perfect "other," warranting Western supremacy and segregation, and vested with exotic mystery. Significant factors in Orientalism are the periodic exclusion of the East from Western gaze and the continual repudiation of the East in favor of the moral and cultural coordinates of the West. The allure of the East has been, in part, based on its impenetrability to the West. The inscrutability attributed to the East is, in fact, the West's failure to achieve full comprehension. Is Western reason, founded in Aristotelian thought, nurtured by Judeo-Christian philosophies of being, and distilled by Cartesian logic and modern rationalism, insufficient when it confronts a culture of alternative customs and ideol-

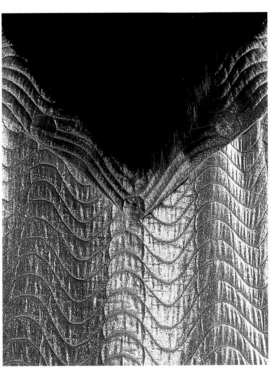

Opposite page and detail above. Jeanne Lanvin. Evening jacket, 1936-37. Silver lamé with black fox trim. Gift of Mrs. Leon L. Roos, 1966 (CI 66.58.1). By the 1930s, the sleek silhouette of the cheongsam had come to represent a *moderne* Orientalism, but the fantasy of Genghis Khan and his Mongol warriors and the feudal extravagance of the Ch'ing court under the last Dowager Empress, Ts'u-hsi, provided opportunities for more dramatic manifestations of a Chinese style.

ogy? Orientalism always challenges the Western mind: it is Orientalism that makes Western culture incomplete and that the West uses to see itself as whole.

Exchange proliferated and empires prospered. In many ways the West was in command. That which was once forbidden to Western gaze was exposed. From the seventeenth until the early nineteenth century, the traders of the British East India Company, as well as the Dutch, Portuguese, and French traffic, attained incalculable wealth. In China Christian missionaries from the West promulgated their cultural and moral code far and wide. In Japan the embargo in effect during the Tokugawa shogunate was ended by Commodore Matthew Perry's uninterdicted entry into Tokyo Bay in 1853. Then followed an immense flow of goods to the West that would play an essential role in determining modern art and design.

Moreover, the East's autonomous moral order beckoned not only those who would convert others but also those who sought to be converted themselves, whether they were ardent travelers in pursuit of non-Western enlightenment or whether they looked for an Eastern model to arouse the West with colorful

9

Charles-Nicholas Cochin. *The Yew Tree Ball* (detail), 1745. Engraving. The Elisha Whittelsey Collection, The Elisha Whittelsey Fund, 1930 (30.22 [34/34]). King Louis XIV and his attendants were dressed as topiary yew trees, while many of the guests arrived in Turquerie or Chinoiserie. But it was the six gargantuan and massively turbaned Turks who best conveyed the exaggerations of the Orientalist vogue.

pageantry and celebration. The ethnic comminglings that inspired eighteenth-century carousels, court masques, and fêtes galantes invariably included elements of Turquerie and Chinoiserie. In early nineteenth-century painting Eugène Delacroix's romantic seraglios and J. A. D. Ingres's irreproachable eroticisms were predicated on that remote place where Western sanctions no longer obtained. In the early twentieth century, European philosopher Mircea Eliade embraced the customs of India. Wearing dhoti and eating with his hands, he became more than a visitor and concluded that in India, "I felt completely at home." In twentieth-century literature, Sebastian Flyte of Evelyn Waugh's novel *Brideshead Revisited* (1945) espoused African exoticism and exile to experience sensations considered taboo in the West.

It is not our purpose to judge colonialism or its international commerce. "These tides of men," to borrow a phrase from the legendary early-twentieth-century Orientalist adventurer T. E. Lawrence (Lawrence of Arabia), embody vast and valid concerns broader and more complex than our modest interests here. Nor do we suspend judgment to endorse touristic enthusiasms, such as the late-nine-

teenth-century writer Lafcadio Hearn's for Japan's "every relation . . . governed by altruism, every action directed by duty and every object shaped by art." Rather, we offer a first inspection of the West's need for and assimilation of the East as evident in apparel.

We know of Western Chinoiserie, Japonisme, and Turquerie as recurring phenomena of the decorative arts and culture. Of the many objects in transaction between East and West, textiles and apparel have been among the most prominent. The power of costume is in its capacity to be absorbed. Nonverbal, the rich textiles and traditions of dress of the East transcend language barriers. The option in dress afforded by the East is charged with enchantment, with a seeming sweetness and seduction that allows the East's presence to seem innocuous. Witness the words of T. E. Lawrence in his letters: "There is a splendid dress called 'of the seven kings': long parallel stripes of the most fiery colours from neck to ankle: it looks glorious; and over that they wear a short blue coat, turned up at the cuffs to show a dull red lining, and they gird themselves with a belt of thirteen vari-colored tassels, and put a black silk & silver weave of Hamath work over their heads under a black goat-hair head-robe. You have then only to add a vest of gold-embroidered silk and white under-tunics to get the idea of one man's dress."

The East, confected from Western desire and imagination, offered a sumptuous wardrobe—clothing to enchant 1,001 nights and to bring to Western dress motives of pagodas, picturesque Asians, an exotic botany, a hermetic and delicate Japan of lacquered and geishaed idyll, a stylized form of the botah that was matrix to the Kashmir and Paisley design and shawls, and many other riches of import and importance. Lawrence of Arabia was unusual in adopting the actual dress of the Arab world as his everyday garb. But, like many other travelers, he also wanted the color, design, and expression afforded by an alien attire that provided not masquerade but revision and choice for the canon of Western dress.

Dress has long expressed an intense multicultur-

Fokine and Fokina in Bakst costumes for *Schéhérazade*, 1910. Dancers from the Ballets Russes in the bejewelled and befeathered costumes from *Schéhérazade* were the benchmark of European Orientalism after the turn of the century. The impact of Diaghilev and his "oriental" Russian company was abetted by the license of modern dance interpretation and a repertory spiced with Orientalist themes.

alism *avant la lettre*. Since the late thirteenth century, when Marco Polo brought the first marvels of China to the West, the East has provided recurrent resuscitation and expansion of Western dress. Can we, however, divorce this process of clothing assimilation and textile adaptation from the politics of hegemonic colonialism? Is dress incriminated in the long, inexorable dossier of economic plunder and the racial presumption of a white West meeting with other worlds and ways? Indisputably, textiles and dress were a part of the economic system that adventuring created and colonialism sustained. Even today, significant manufacture for Western markets occurs on sites once known as the East. One cannot exculpate clothing from these cultural and economic destinies and defilements. But one can realize that clothing has served to consolidate more than to segregate. While never losing the characteristics of its place of origin, clothing has shown itself a readily assimilated object. The foreignness of the exotic is more easily forgiven in clothing, perhaps because we tend to think of clothing as less fixed to place and less calibrated to long life. Portability and ephemerality promote investigation, at the very least. Eastern ideas of textile, design, construction, and utility have been realized again and again as a positive contribution to the culture of the West. The West has tested Eastern materials and ideas in dress and has approved and immediately assimilated them, often faddishly.

It is clothing—so close to and expressive of the body—that the West has most joyously appropriated from the East. The guilt of body difference, racial intolerance, and exploitation that has customarily defined the discussion of colonialism as a political strategy would seem to inhibit any exchanges in clothing if bodies are, in fact, perceived so differently and so hierarchically. Any presumption of body supremacy and racial prerogative would seem to be mitigated by a constant Western history of assimilating global dress. Of course, the process of assimilation was on the West's terms and safely within the West's own precinct. The explorers and missionaries kept steadfastly to the standards and scruples of

Madame Paul Poiret and a guest at the Poiret's 1002nd Night, 1911. Poiret's charismatic inventiveness established many fashion ideas. Long before the era of media, Poiret created in a widely-reported event that was the single most important fashion party of the century. Mme Poiret is here pictured in a turban and the flared overskirt, or lampshade tunic, that was so widely noted.

Western dress, often with ludicrous resistance to geographical difference. While "going native" in attire was taboo to those in the field, the inventory of trade goods and the travelogue of images that returned to Europe and America promoted the possibilty of Eastern dress to those who stayed at home. Thus, the body transference may have ended symbolically somewhere at the importer's trade counter or the adaptor's workroom. The voyager's risk and the missionary's impropriety would be to actually wear the foreign garment. By the time the concept appeared in Western design, its source was not forgotten, but its body was undeniably Western.

A significant means by which images of Eastern dress were disseminated was the costume plate, which became universal in the nineteenth century. Fashion exemplars were found throughout the East in these illustrations of fashion styles that gave images of mandarins and samurai a status equivalent to that attributed earlier to the noble figures of classical antiquity. Arguably, this new repertory of imagery, which had thoroughly replaced the histori-cal Western sources of most earlier editions of fashion plates by the 1850s, was a reference of style images that could be consulted at any time or place in the West.

Thus, the Orientalist objective in Western dress was to cull from the various Easts their spellbinding foreignness for the purposes of rendering Western dress richer and more exotic. In the seventeenth and eighteenth centuries the Western wardrobe was vastly enriched by the sumptuous stuffs of the East that brought new pattern and possibility to Western dress, even as it was immediately copied by mills in England and France. In the nineteenth century, the era of universal expositions and colonial exchange brought object categories, such as silks from China, shawls from India, or, after 1854, kimono from Japan, into the West, and created businesses of copying and adaptation that used Western monikers such as "Paisley" and "moderne" to conceal the blatantness of the imitations. Thus, the French journal *L'Illustration* (July 20, 1867) claimed with bravado of the Paris Universal Exposition, "Dreamers of travels, those who are attached by the short chain of their jobs and who dream of excursions on the banks of the Nile or Bosphorus . . . now have no reason to complain. If they cannot go to the Orient, the Orient has come to them." With the fashions of Poiret early in the twentieth century, Western structure was modified by the intervention of the East; it would shortly be altered in architecture as well.

We cannot conceive of dress today without the East. The worlds some sought to conquer, others strove to exploit, and yet others tried to convert have overwhelmed that little domain of England and the European continent that once thought it was the world or at least the world's designated leader. Dress has never been apolitical; but it has been portable, and as one of the art forms most susceptible to new knowledge and expanded horizons, it has accommodated a changing world. Thus, clothing is predisposed to tell us something of our conventions and inventions, our inhibitions and ambitions. The vista of the East has altered Western life and dress. The world view of East and West reconciled in mutuality

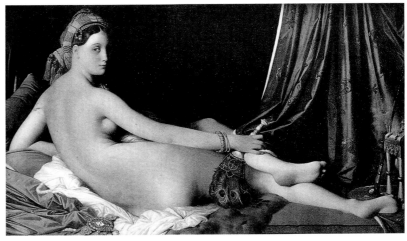

Left: Carl Van Loo. *The Trusted Friend* (detail), ca. 1750. Musée des Arts Décoratifs, Paris. A portrait said to be of Mme de Pompadour not only depicts her in Oriental-style dress but places her in the suggestive setting of Orientalist relaxation. The servant girl with coffee pot underscores the painting's Turkish conceit. Right: Jean-Auguste-Dominique Ingres. *La Grande Odalisque*, 1814. Oil on canvas. Musée du Louvre, Paris. The Orientalist female was a fabrication of the West, attributing Salambô-like license and nudity to figures who escaped Occidental sanction by their placement in an Orientalist world. The male gaze and the imperial gaze were demonstrably linked, and the servitude of colonials and women alike placed them on a level patently beneath that of the Western male.

is a vision today as beguiling as the bygone perception of a remote and romantic world, exotically dressed, was in earlier times.

In fact, clothing is always political and even prone to its own missionary conversions through its systems of generating signs and values. The dress of the East, perceived and translated by the West, was no less volatile. Trade and colonialism were founded on silk roads and transactions in textiles. The wealth of many nations has depended on textiles, whose design and embellishment reify national and international values. World's fairs, expositions, and commercial displays have consistently sought to bring the East to the West in one of its most portable and persuasive forms, clothing. It would always be possible to build Chinoiserie teahouse follies in royal gardens, such as Frederick the Great's Sans Souci at Potsdam (1754-57) and its successive Chinese-inspired gardens, but the soil remained European, and the large effect was one of declaimed exoticism.

In addition to the great textiles, ideas of Eastern dress have come to be a part of Western dress, including saris and dhotis from India, kimonos from Japan, caftans and djellabahs from North Africa, and cheongsam from China. The East offers a larger concept in alternative to the Western propensity for tailoring. In giving primacy to the textile, Eastern dress emphasizes the flat terrain of cloth, the looping and wrapping of the garment, and the integrity of the untailored textile. These values, antithetical to postmedieval Western dress, have offered a paradigm of dressing and dressmaking to the West that has been sporadically influential, and notably so in our time.

The explorers searched. The missionaries cajoled. The traders swapped and marketed. Europe would be forever changed by its East. Silk roads brought to the West goods of indescribable luxury and beauty, but they also brought a new looking glass for fashion and thus for life and even for self-confidence. G. K. Chesterton remarked of a popular Gilbert and Sullivan operetta (1885), "There is not, the whole length of *The Mikado*, a single joke that is a joke against Japan. They are all . . . jokes against England . . . . *The Mikado* is not a picture of Japan; but it is a Japanese picture."

Orientalism is not a picture of the East or the Easts. It represents longing, option, and faraway perfection. It is, like Utopia, a picture everywhere and nowhere, save in the imagination.

China

Cathay was the name for China in the Middle Ages. It was a land outside the reach of most travelers, but the world of Kublai Khan could be attained just barely, by only the most intrepid. Those few returned home with their hoards, fables, and desires and reported their stories of the civilization that had purposefully excluded the West and now glittered with wealth, sophistication, and power.

Romance attached to Cathay. At the turn-of-the-nineteenth century, British poet Samuel Taylor Coleridge described the far-off land and its colorful history. Coleridge's Xanadu is a fictive place, an acculturated version of an East of magic and mystery, though remembered in part from travelers' accounts. Its differences from the capitals of the West bestow on it a quaint charm, even while its similarities offer an inspiration akin to a vision of heaven. Long had the enchantment of Cathay held thrall from the accounts of traders and preeminently of Marco Polo, always with the possibility that these extravagant and exotic images might be vitiated by exaggeration or even by total fabrication. By 1368, there was no choice but to believe the tales, as China was closed to Western traders and its lure persisted only in the ever-growing legend. On the

Opposite page and detail above. French. Court gown, 1760s. Cloth-of-silver brocaded with silver lace trim. Gift of the Fédération de la Soirie, 1950 (50.168.2 a,b). Western Chinoiserie is often a compound of exotic elements, not all indigenous to China. This eighteenth-century dress exhibits such multiple allusions, but they have been assimilated by the technology and aesthetic of the Lyonnais manufacture. Palm trees signify the foreign, and the pagoda-inspired follies depicted are posts with tented swags, an Eastern architecture transplanted to the West.

collapse of the Ming Dynasty in the seventeenth century, when trade resumed and artifacts flowed West again, the prized commodities that had to travel so far to the Italian port cities and to Portugal, England, and Holland were the most portable, and most telling of the East's customs and culture. Easiest of all such products to import because of their relatively light weight, import textiles from China prompted fascination with the technical skills involved in the weaving, hand-painting, and needlework of Chinese silk. Textiles were accompanied by other luxury objects. The porcelains carried to the West in the same period provided depictions that showed the West how costume was worn in China.

Almost without exception, the precious cloth was readily made into Western tailored garments. Thus, a French eighteenth-century cloth-of-silver dress is identifiably of the period, recognizable by its silhouette—with extended center-back pleats from neckline to hem and panniered lateral extension—and by its floral pattern. Amidst rococo roses, however, reside pagodas and palm trees. These are as fashionably present as they are in Georgian design, "Chinese Chippendale" mid-eigh-

Jean Mariette (after Jean Bérain). Design for a Chinese masquerade costume worn by the duc de Bourgogne, ca. 1700. Engraving. Courtesy Bibliothèque Nationale, Paris. The presence of authentic elements of Eastern dress is more surprising than the creative distortion of this Western artist and costumer for the court of Louis XIV. The undiluted persistence of the ethnographically real is symptomatic of eighteenth-century European festival and fancy-dress costume, which though based on factual data was transformed by distance and the frequently embellished reports of travelers.

France. The style was one of ebullient reconciliations, not the least of which was East with West.

In other instances, one discerns immediately that the product made in China for an export market has been altered by the West, shaped into Western form. Eighteenth-century painted silks demonstrate a true interweaving of two vastly contrasting cultures; after all, the development from textile to clothing is a process very different from the importation of porcelains or the inspiration of architectural examples. An intact artifact of China can become the constituent or the raw material of a cooked Western end product, never entirely sacrificing its integrity to the assimilated end result. Of course, a technique borrowed in one example can stimulate like efforts, and Europe did not merely secure textiles from China; it also copied them. In a seventeenth-century cape the Chinese techniques are as identifiable as any other sign of place of origin.

The faraway dream of Cathay and of forbidden cities suggested to the European imagination a set of ceremonies and court life to rival those of Europe. Little was known of the Chinese court, and its ritual was therefore concocted in fable and reified in images purporting to depict the most magnificent and densely peopled festivals and rites. Thus, images of full-dress ceremony could appear stately in the manner of the eighteenth century or of the first half of the nineteenth century. After the Prince of Wales (later George IV) had the Brighton Pavilion built in the 1780s, the extravagance of exotic fabrication seemed capricious and profligate, discordant with the intense economic matters of empire. Likewise, textiles assumed a new sobriety. By the 1850s, however, exoticism was tempered increasingly by an ethnographic respect and accuracy, as the bourgeoisie that was looking for an East beyond formal gardens and enigmatic ceremonial pomp sought and delighted in a bona-fide Chinoiserie. In ceramics and in architecture scholarship and connoisseurship were fostering a more academic and accurate replication of the Chinese design forms. An at-home dress of the 1850s is characteristic of this nineteenth-century change in attitude. The ebullient and

teenth-century furniture, Jean-Baptiste Pillement's fantasies, and the colorful wallpapers with Chinese themes that adorned Enlightenment boudoirs. In fact, much of the most heroic Chinoiserie of the era entered the European imagination gleefully and capriciously through the Anglo-Chinese garden plan with its formality and fanciful pagodas and through intimate interiors with handpainted wallpaper animated by Chinoiserie narratives, imaginative botanicals, and passages of fictive Chinese architecture. As Dawn Jacobson, in her book *Chinoiserie* (1992) has pointed out, variety was a liberating factor of the Rococo taste, especially in inventive Chinoiserie of earlier times now became a deliberate and self-conscious use of Chinese materials and symbols. Floral medallions might not be taken in the West to be direct symbols of China, but they were surely locatable to the constraint and gravity characteristic of China. To wear Chinese dress at home was not a frivolous and fanciful gesture; it was an imperial act, signifying worldly knowledge. As Edward Said has shown convincingly in his book *Culture and Imperialism*, Charles Dickens's *Great Expectations* (1861) is a novel about the English relationship to the exotic. Even if it is read as an allegory of colonial acceptance—complicated by Australia's dual identity as British penal institution and as exotic land—the nineteenth-century paradox between nativism embraced and colonial peoples held at arm's length is evident. Even the British East India Company's monopoly in the China trade had ceased in 1834. China's independence was a particular advantage: a possible colonial posting did not mitigate the exoticism; China always had to be reckoned with, if not as an equal, at least as a free party and an alternative.

The peculiar trait of China among Orientalisms to be more equitable—inasmuch as it was never conquered and colonized—has promoted the role of China in the twentieth century. Often affiliated with the avant-garde, China was the Orientalism that most readily became a part of European hybrid culture, its obsessiveness and ardor often encompassing many Eastern traits under the rubric of China. Thus, the confusion in the nineteenth century of some Japonisme—even in the case of Claude Monet's famous painting *Garden at Sainte-Adresse* (1867)—with authentic Chinese influences continued into the twentieth century and sur-

J.B. Martin. Ballet Costume: Chinese Man, 1779. *Galerie des Modes.* A costume condenses the several certain signs of the Chinese in the eighteenth century, including a pagoda-shaped hat, batwing-like lapels, meandering tree patterns, and faux-Chinese script.

J.B. Martin. Ballet Costume: Chinese Woman, 1779. *Galerie des Modes.* A companion costume shows a woman wearing a gown with pagoda sleeves. Almost anything that flared in the eighteenth-century dress, whether hat or sleeve or collar, was called *en pagode.* Reversed scallops as seen along the neckline alluded as well to an Orientalist taste.

French. Open robe with matching petticoat, late 18th century. Hand-painted green-and-white woven striped silk taffeta. Purchase, Irene Lewisohn Bequest, 1954 (CI 54.70 a,b). The sprig-floral patterning and stripping of this painted silk, exported from China and consummated by a Western dressmaker, reflects a purely Western sensibility. In this instance, an object created for the export market addresses a non-Chinese taste, though the concept of the painted silk textile and its execution are Chinese. Further, the Western dressmaker gives the garment the European silhouette of the period—with the continuous back pleat from neckline to train—that is so frequently represented in the contemporaneous paintings of Antoine Watteau.

rounded Poiret's innovative fashions, which were equally cited by European and American critics as Chinese, North African, or Middle Eastern. Even the work of Callot Soeurs in the 1920s, with its Chinese gowns so fully attuned to the Art Deco environment, was an accommodation to Western techniques of embroidery and decoration. Earlier wallpapers and porcelains could be parsed to distinguish discrete Chinese influences, or at least the signal dragons and coolie figures and pagodas on them could. Lafcadio Hearn, enthusiast for Japan, once said that Japan was indescribable to the Occident; the explicability of the various Easts in the twentieth-century accounts for their fusion into a single entity in the Western eye and mind. In fact, the references in twentieth-century dress to Chinese porcelains and coromandel screens could be construed as a kind of clarifying gesture, an attempt to guarantee that China is the explicit source, after the long interminglings of the different Easts that had been elements in Chinese-ascribed dress.

The imagining of China was always more fanciful than real. Trade provided products, but even more

La Toilette Chinoise, 1814. *Le Bon Genre*. Accompanied by a text that explains "Chinese styles incessantly reappear in Paris," this plate documents many of the decorative effects, including dagging and saw-toothed hems that could be ascribed to a variety of historical and geographical sources, Chinese, Tudor, Renaissance, and Turkish. The certainty was not of specific origin but of an alien world.

importantly, the West copied the Oriental land that it had never conquered. It never possessed the dragons, butterflies, or pagodas that it admired and emulated. If it was an unrequited colonialism, the West's passion for China abides today in the continuing aesthetic fascination for that Far Eastern land.

Jeanne Lanvin. Evening dress and bolero, summer 1927. Black taffeta partially embroidered with silver thread, paillettes, and sequins. Gift of Mme Yves Lanvin, 1960 (CI 60.19 a,b). A Chinoiserie decorative motif on a vest is married to the signature Lanvin *robe de style*. Consonant with the Lanvin silhouette, the dress selectively borrows from the East, almost in the manner of a Chinoiserie object placed in a modernist interior as a point of punctuation. "Throughout her collections," wrote Caroline Rennolds Milbank of Lanvin, "embroideries appear that are reminiscent of Aztec, Renaissance, eighteenth-century, Impressionist, or Cubist art. Whereas another couturière might have been tempted to translate these elements literally, Lanvin's taste and vision were so strong that they became instantly 'hers.'"

Horst. *Mrs. Reginald Fellowes, Bal Oriental*, 1935. Photograph © Horst. Created in the 1920s, the cheongsam is an icon of modern China and was originally a symbol of emancipated women. This everyday dress—in cotton or, more often, in silk—became high-style eveningwear when appropriated by the West. In the 1930s, the cheongsam came to signify Chinese dress, and even Hollywood movies of the period confirmed it as the identifying garb of Chinese women.

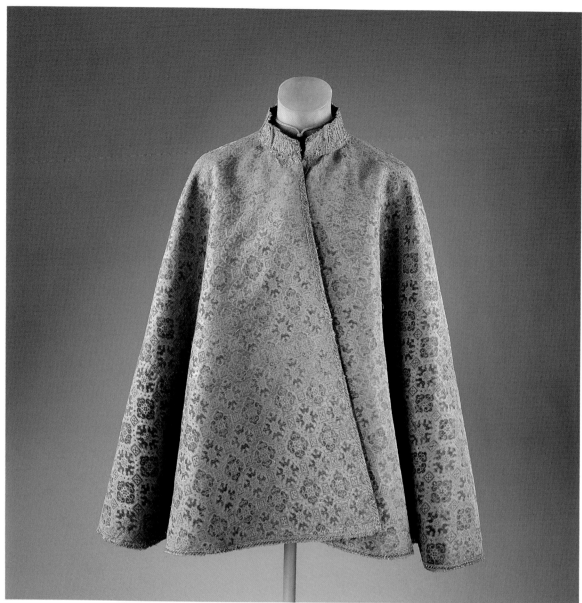

Portuguese. Man's cape, late 17th century. Brocaded gold silk velvet embroidered with metal-wrapped thread. Gift of J. Pierpont Morgan, 1906 (06.941). This mantle, made with Ming Dynasty Chinese velvet, is purely European in form. The textile's gold thread is of a typical Chinese style: gilded paper wound on a core of orange silk.

Opposite page. English. At-home dress, ca. 1850. Chinese aubergine silk damask and velvet. Purchase, Judith and Gerson Leiber Fund, 1994 (1994.302.1). An at-home dress, made of Chinese patterned silk, uses an export textile in a Western garment. Arguably, Asian textiles were associated in the Western mind as much with private leisure as with ceremony. Many Eastern textiles entered Western dress first as intimate boudoir and other at-home garments such as robes and banyans, suggesting the qualities of exoticism and erotic mystery associated with far-off lands. The selvage at the back waist reveals Chinese characters indicating the textile's manufacture, and the flaring sleeves are what the West calls the pagoda style.

Opposite page. Left: French. Robe à la Polonaise (open robe and matching petticoat), ca. 1780. Hand-painted white Chinese silk. Purchase, Mr. and Mrs. Alan S. Davis Gift, 1976 (1976.146.a,b). Right: American. Robe à la Polonaise, 1780-85. Hand-painted yellow Chinese silk. Gift of Heirs of Emily Kearney Rodgers Cowenhoven, 1970 (1970.87 a,b). Russian, German, and French Rococo styles absorbed Chinoiserie into a seamless whole of *frivoles*, fêtes galantes, and colorful narratives. One particular syncretism is evident in painted wallpapers and dress where the traditional Western floral forms in Rococo taste cross-pollinated with meandering patterns of profoundly Chinese effect.

François Hubert Drouais. *Madame de Pompadour*, 1763-64. Oil on canvas. National Gallery, London. Photograph: Bridgeman/Art Resource, New York. Mme de Pompadour was the great patron of the Sèvres porcelain factories—which, in 1753, became "manufacture royale de porcelaine"—in their production, and to some degree reproduction, of Chinese styles, especially blanc-de-chine ware. Thus, while this portrait of Mme de Pompadour wearing a painted-silk dress is unusual for its documentation of the exotic textile, the taste for Chinoiserie that it portrays was well established.

Opposite page. Jeanne Hallée. Dress, 1907. Black silk crepe embroidered with silk floss and ribbon. Gift of Howard Sturges, in memory of his mother, Mrs. Howard O. Sturges, 1949 (CI 49.2.5). In an ingenious fusion of Art Nouveau and the palette, line, and specific motives of Chinoiserie, a blue-and-white cloud pattern is isolated at the shoulder in the manner of Manchu court robes. The embroidery with its satin-stitch floats has the effulgent appearance of Chinese prototypes.

The Pagoda, 1914. *Costumes Parisiennes.* The pagoda became the most pervasive and easily recognizable symbol of China in the West. In the teens, dress emulated the tiered form, as the shifting silhouette moved away from the body and became an abstracted tube or cone comparable to the axioms of Cubism and Futurism. Poiret's melded exoticism could evoke China, Japan, or the Near East with the same ambiguity by which first perceptions of Monet's *Garden at St. Adresse* could describe it as either a Chinese (as Monet himself called it) or, more accurately, a Japanese view. A-line shapes of Middle Eastern and Turkish garments could seem indistinguishable from the metaphor of the pagoda.

25

Opposite page. Left: Callot Soeurs. Evening dress, ca. 1924. Pale-green silk satin embroidered with silk floss and gold metal-wrapped thread. Gift of Isabel Shults, 1944 (CI 44.64.10). Right: Callot Soeurs. Evening dress, ca. 1926. Blue silk satin embroidered with silk floss. Gift of Isabel Shults, 1946 (CI 46.64.14 a,b). In a sense, the work of Callot Soeurs in the 1920s deflated the nineteenth-century silhouette, while distilling the sumptuous materials of dress. The tubular modernism of the Callot Soeurs is a contrast of structural reduction and ornamental play, with motifs similar to those seen in the Chinese export shawls popular in the 1920s.

LA BELLE PERSONNE
ROBE DU SOIR, DE WORTH

George Barbier. *La Belle Personne: Robe du Soir de Worth*, 1925. *Gazette du bon ton*. The 1920s taste for a lustrous, minimalist, highly colorful Chinoiserie is well exemplified by this dress, which shows evident kinship to a lac-de-chine commode or coromandel screen. Moreover, the *Gazette du bon ton* illustration characteristically places the garment in an aesthetic environment, a profligate array of essentially chaste Chinese taste.

Opposite page. Premet. Evening coat, 1928–29. Gold lamé heavily embroidered with blue glass beads. Gift of Marie Sterner Lintott, 1949 (CI 49.52). The confluence of Egyptomania, Japonisme, and Chinoiserie under the reductive rubric of Art Deco that occurred in the 1920s resulted in an intoxicating confusion of exoticisms. The tiered landscape with straw-hatted figures that appears on this evening coat resembles the picturesque Cathay portrayed on blue-and-white Chinese porcelain.

Valentino. Dress and overtunic, fall–winter 1993. Black silk satin and cotton lace with seed bead embroidery. Courtesy Valentino. A Valentino outfit is close in overall effect to a Chinese jacket, but the designer's use of black lace and beading is surprising and differentiates the contemporary garment from its several possible sources. Valentino does not practice a Chinoiserie of replication but rather one of assimilated select elements and of combined cultural vocabularies.

Valentino. Suit, fall–winter 1990-91. Beige silk chiffon embroidered in red-and-gold sequins. Courtesy Valentino. "I react like a painter," describes Valentino of his sources. "All manner of things may attract me: Hungary, Bavaria in Ludwig's day, China, or some kitschy show I happened to see in a faraway land. But the result will not so closely resemble the thing that inspired it." Thus, Valentino's 1990s exoticism of signs—pagodas and palms— is visually knowledgeable but not strictly studious, based less on Chinese costume than on Chinese and Japanese lacquers.

Agnès Drecoll. Evening gown and bolero, 1932–38. Blue-gray wool crepe and orange silk crepe embroidered with silk floss and metal-wrapped thread. Gift of Miss Julia P. Wightman, 1990 (1990.104.11 a–c). The combination of coral and turquoise suggests a Chinese palette, and the embroidery at the bodice and bolero is directly inspired by the borders of Manchu court gowns. By the 1930s, advanced Chinese-Deco taste was characterized by a sinuous decoration of meandering bands and borders in the colors of Chinese porcelains and embroidery.

Left: Yves Saint Laurent. Evening jacket, fall–winter 1977–78. Quilted red silk satin with gold trim. Courtesy Yves Saint Laurent. Right: Yves Saint Laurent. Evening jacket, fall–winter 1977–78. Black silk velvet embroidered with gold. Courtesy Yves Saint Laurent. "I returned," said Saint Laurent in 1977 of his fall–winter China collection, "to an age of elegance and wealth. In many ways I returned to my own past." Like his scent "Opium," launched in the same year, the China collection affirmed the designer's strong Eastern sensibility. Saint Laurent uses the Chinese patterning device of stacked scallops (fish scales or the banded wave borders of Ch'ing court robes), a technique of quilting associated with Chinese winter jackets, pagoda sleeves, tassels, and the colors of the Chinese opera.

Left: Dolce & Gabbana. Evening
ensemble, fall–winter 1992–93.
Brocaded orange silk satin. Courtesy
Dolce & Gabbana. Right: Byron
Lars. Evening ensemble, 1994.
Brocaded red satin, black satin.
Courtesy Wheaton International. In
the 1990s, Orientalism has entered
the hyperbolic vocabulary of post-
modern design. Frog closures
formed by zippers, for example,
suggest both the original source and
its appropriation into new form.
Bustier and bomber jacket motives
coexist with eminently legible
Orientalist elements. Avoiding
parody, but nonetheless showing
heightened awareness of sources,
post-modern Orientalism
acknowledges the abiding renown
of imagined Easts.

India

"Posh," our word for the smart, elegant, and luxurious, is the acronym of the British voyage to India. The trip departed from Tilbury or Southampton and arrived in Bombay and carried the assurance that the passenger would dodge the cruelest sun by booking passage port going and starboard home. Similar journeys by the East India Company had brought immense wealth to England and the European continent. India was a major international resource for textiles, especially cotton (and chintz in particular) and wool and supplied the growing appetites of both England and continental Europe for these commodities. During the long period of imperialism, India supplied the West with extraordinary models for dress, often by way of military apparel. In fashion, however, three articles of Indian dress have had enduring effect: the banyan, the sari, and the Kashmir shawl. Each remained indigenous to India, and each was rapaciously exploited by the European fashion industries.

The Indian-house gown, sometimes conflated with cognate Turkish robes, became the model for eighteenth-century banyans in

Opposite page and detail of robe à l'Anglaise above. Left: French. Evening dress, ca. 1810. White mull with allover embroidery with silver tinsel. Gift of Mrs. Langdon Marvin, 1976 (1976.137.1). Right: French. Robe à l'Anglaise (open robe and matching petticoat), ca. 1784-87. White muslin embroidered with silver-colored metallic tinsel. Isabel Shults Fund, 1991 (1991.204 a,b). Cotton emerged as a fashionable fabric in the 1780s with the chemise à la reine, the cotton shift favored as dress by Marie Antoinette beginning in this turbulent decade. As always, clothing had political and international implications. One of the chief reasons the Lyons silk manufacturers railed against the reductive, modern attire is that their luxurious silks were being abandoned in favor of imported cottons from India. The textile of the robe à l'Anglaise demonstrates its origin in a metallic gold selvage with red weaver's mark.

Europe. This popular form of informal dress for men seized at-home and post-prandial socialization as the perfect opportunity for an untailored garment that would loosen the otherwise rigid silhouette of men's eighteenth-century attire. In fact, after removing their jackets to be represented wearing banyans, men of the period generally retained their waistcoats. They were then depicted in a state of ease that was otherwise a thorough anomaly of men's tailored attire. Even today, Indian references and paisley textiles abound in men's dressing gowns and robes, so consistent and purposeful is the sense of Indian tradition in these garments. The banyan was a paradigm of men's clothing that was neither bedclothes nor an acceptable street apparel. It marked the beginning of the use of intermediate forms of dress that would attempt to mediate between formal dress (as initially determined by courts and later by business) and casual dress (once marginal but continually expanded until profligate in twentieth-century apparel). In the 1780s, when the banyan first was seen in public, it was the counterpart of the Indian cottons of the chemise à la

English. Man's banyan, ca. 1735, brown figured silk faille.
Purchase, Irene Lewisohn Fund, 1981 (1981.208.2). In contrast to
the narrow back, tight sleeve, and fitted torso of male dress in
the eighteenth century, the banyan provided an ease of cut that
popularized its use as undress. Its simple "T" shape reflects its
source in untailored regional traditions.

Le Clerc. Robe de Chambre, 1780. *Galerie des Modes*. Smoking and
coffee were the exotic, Eastern habits that enthralled the West. A
banyan with pagoda sleeves could be the apt accompaniment in
dress. The result is the synthetic East: Turkish coffee, an Indian-
style banyan, and Chinese pagoda sleeves. The counterfeit is not
in the parts, but in the combination that the West derives.

reine, once an undergarment until worn, with the
sanction of Marie Antoinette, as dress in faintly
evolved form.

If the banyan was a wrapping, sheathing garment
for men, the sari was the more persuasive wrap in
Indian attire offered as a choice to Western dress.
Like other Orientalist options, the sari's primary
alternative is the dress with an aversion to cut, a single continuous cloth swaddling the body in opposi-
tion to the more frequent complications of Western
patternmaking. Treated as textiles, saris have been
cannibalized from as early as the late eighteenth century to conform to prevailing Western styles. Their

recurrence as a model for Western dress is only
recently associated directly with the vernacular dress
of India. Even in sympathetic renderings of the sari,
its draped form has often been confused with the
toga and classicism. Madame Grès's deliberate use of
the sari (both before and after her 1958 sojourn in
India), for example, was subsumed under her abiding
interest in a pleated columnarity resembling images
of classical dress.

Inescapably, though, it is the historical and continuing influence of the Kashmir shawl and its pattern, the botah or paisley, a stylized form of foliate
and floral decoration that has been most enduringly

adopted. Wool shawls made in Kashmir of the abstracted pattern of the botah—at first in isolated bands of ornament and later in a horror vacuii profusion—became the vogue in Europe in the last third of the eighteenth century. By early in the nineteenth century, these elegant shawls provided the perfect accent to both the relatively reduced forms of dress and the physical lightening of their textiles and decoration. In a sense, a shawl is the incomplete version of the unconstructed and wrapped garment. Because of the relative ease of the smaller piece of fabric and its utility in complementing and completing the major understructures of the European silhouette, the Kashmir shawl prevailed as a colorful accessory redolent of its distant origins.

"Your amir," says the native officer in Rudyard Kipling's *The Jungle Book*, "must come here and take orders from our Viceroy." Kipling knew that power proceeds from the top. Empires being what they are, the Paisley shawl demonstrates the economic exploitation of a commodity by the imperial power. The shawls imported from India were so highly prized that the venal and competitive spirit of Europe was aroused. The production of similar shawls was undertaken in Lyons and in Scotland, the latter in the town and region of Paisley. So avid was the consumption of the Scottish production that the name Kashmir was changed to Paisley. Thus, the pattern was not only flagrantly and brusquely swindled from the colony; even its name was usurped. Some European-made Paisley shawls found their way back to India. The shawl's presence at world's fairs and expositions furthered its impact in Europe and America through the mid-nineteenth century. By this time, its increasingly elaborated motifs represented a complication of profuse pattern almost akin to engineering plans. By the late nineteenth century, what began as a faddish exoticism had been integrated completely into Western tradition.

Because the shawl is an accessory of dress rather than a principal garment, its popularity persisted despite the vagaries of fashion and the accelerated changes in women's dress in the nineteenth century. Further, its prolix design might have been wearisome to a Western taste that often veers capriciously from vogue to vogue, but its secondary role allowed even its most elaborate patterns to be acceptable and beyond fad. As always, the Orientalist features of the garment—a cut undifferentiated as to sex, a decontextualized patterning that has lost any gender identification—allow it to be used by either men or women. What would have been attire for both men and women in India became an accessory of dress exclusively for women in England and the rest of Europe. Ironically, the paisley pattern was sustained in European and American use in the twentieth century principally

John Singleton Copley. *Joseph Sherburne*, ca. 1767-70. The Metropolitan Museum of Art, Amelia B. Lazarus Fund, 1923 (23.143). Samuel Pepys rented his banyan when he sat for his portrait in order to be depicted in the style of gentlemanly ease. The American colonies, even before independence, manifested an informality, though one descended from such English examples. An American might have recognized the banyan's Indian origin but would have affected it primarily because it was English.

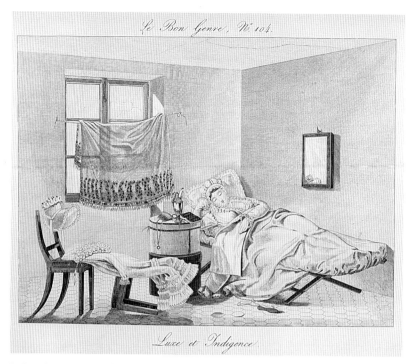

Le Bon Genre, 1811. For the exaggerated styles of Merveilleuse excess and Incroyable indulgence after the French Revolution, the ultimate accessory was the Kashmir shawl.

Le Bon Genre, 1817. In this print inscribed "Luxe et Indigence," the Kashmir shawl, which has plunged the modish Parisienne into destitution, displays a novel utility.

in menswear as a form now perceived as traditionally Anglo-Saxon.

One other garment type, the dhoti, the Hindu trousers for men with a band of cloth passed through the legs, had some resonance in European dress, inspiring dress reformers and twentieth-century designers.

Of course, India offered countless resources in textiles, including muslin and cotton madras and cottons acquired in China and passed through the East India Company to England and Europe. Ironically, the fine textiles that had been an attraction for pre-industrialized India in the eighteenth century waned as cheaper, industrial-grade textiles took their place not only in Europe, but even in India's markets in South Asia as well. The local, handicraft character of Indian textile production—both Muslim and Hindu—was vexing to the needs of the European market for standardized production. Later, homespun clothing and cap—the caste-

less Gujurat head covering that became known as the Gandhi cap—and the spinning wheel became marks for Indian nationalism under Mohandas Gandhi, these standing for a consolidated India unlike the regional textile types that had preceded.

Thus, both Gandhi and Nehru in seriatim offered dress as symbolic resistance and identification with the people in a land where clothing had already been used and expropriated to serve empire.

In fact, for all their oppression, empires betokened a kind of freedom in apparel. Colonials might wear only European dress for ceremonial and public occasions, but they could find relaxation and escape in the seemingly less formal attire of the East. Thus, when carried to the West, Orientalist dress was most often found first in lounging, smoking, and other private contexts. When the British in India returned home, it was with a richness of textile and an even greater plethora of clothing options, a baggage that defined "posh."

Jean-Auguste-Dominique Ingres. *Madame Jacques Louis Leblanc (Francoise Poncelle)*, 1823. Catharine Lorillard Wolfe Collection, Wolfe Fund, 1918 (19.77.2). In the nineteenth century, the women of Europe donned imported-from-India Kashmir shawls with abandon. The vivid, complex designs served as accents during a period of monochromatic European dress. The Kashmir shawl became a hallmark of wealth and fashionability, persisting almost throughout the nineteenth century, even as copies made in England and France came into use.

Carraceni. Man's lounging jacket, 1964. Nineteenth-century paisley wool shawl. Gift of Valerian Stux Rybar, 1974 (1974.255 a). In this instance, a nineteenth-century shawl, turned wrong side out, has been remade into a Nehru jacket. The Nehru style enjoyed popularity as menswear in the 1960s, in part as a sign of approval of modern India's democratic and progressive spirit under Nehru. In the Mod and early hippie period, global exoticism, especially when inflected with the spiritual, affected dress and introduced Native American, Eastern, and African elements to the clothing vocabulary of both men and women.

Right. Christian Bérard. Schiaparelli's spiral saris, 1935. In the 1930s, many French couturiers, including Grès, Rochas, and Schiaparelli, were profoundly influenced by Asian dress, often as a consequence of the international expositions that took place in Europe. Not only was the sari considered exotic during the period, it also fed into the contemporaneous fascination with bias draping. Thus, the bias drape created by the sari's spiral path over the body used an Eastern practice in accord with a new Western interest.

Below left. Left: Christian Dior. Evening dress, fall 1953. White silk satin embroidered with gold bugle beads, sequins and thread. Gift of Mrs. Byron C. Foy, 1955 (55.76.14 a-c). Right: Pierre Balmain. Evening gown, 1953. Gray peau de soie embroidered with gold braid, polychrome sequins and pearls. Gift of Jean Sinclair Tailer, 1964 (64.13.2). Like many Eastern exoticisms, Indian Orientalism in dress is often composed of elements of the decorative arts mingled with motives endemic to apparel.

Below right: Mainbocher. Evening dress, mid 1950s. Pale peach silk embroidered with silver thread. Gift of Mrs. Deane F. Johnson, 1973 (1973.42). Inventive in fabric choices throughout his career, Mainbocher was intrigued by the sari's construction and cloth. In this example, he uses Indian export silk with brocaded borders in the manner of sari fabric. As with Japan in the second half of the nineteenth century, postwar India encouraged export in a similar impulse toward international economic development.

40

Gottex. Topkapi bathing suit and coverup, 1989. Silk-screened red synthetic jersey. Courtesy Gottex Industries. A printed pattern replicates Sind and Gujurat mirror cloth, which is actually composed of embroidery stitches with bits of glass. Thus, the contemporary adaptation seizes the graphic power of the original cloth but simplifies its creation. Furthermore, the surprising displacement from festive dress to swimwear extends the role of modification.

French. Robe à l'Anglaise (open robe and matching petticoat), third quarter of 18th century. Printed ivory cotton. Purchase, Irene Lewisohn Bequest, 1964 (CI 64.32.3 a,b). An exotic floral pattern alludes to Pillement's Chinoiserie patterns. The French fabric interprets an Indian export fabric that itself was a copy of what was considered a Chinese pattern. Thus characteristic of the tissued complexity of "exotic" sources, Orientalism is never a narrow-gauge or scholastic enterprise in fashion. Rather, it is a fantasy, often a composite and customarily synthesized.

Opposite page. Left: American or European. Day dress, ca. 1850. Floral-patterned cream silk gauze. Gift of Miss Claire Lorraine Wilson, 1942 (CI 42.76.3 a,b). Right: American or European. Afternoon dress, ca. 1855. Paisley-printed off-white silk organdy with woven satin stripe. Gift of University of Virginia Drama Department, 1977 (1977.304.1). Nineteenth-century gauze dresses incorporate the romance of the buta motif in fabrics that have no similarity to the original Kashmiri wools. The endemic and indivisible Paisley-wool ligature is dissociated in the West, chiefly because of its extraordinary popularity as it becomes a design motif for all seasons. By the twentieth century, paisley, in the West, came to be associated as much with silk and cotton—notably in home furnishings and men's neckties—as with wool.

French. *Le Lion*, July 1857. Supplement to *L'Elegant*. The tasseled cap and skirted gown *à la Turque* with double sleeves introduced a more fitted silhouette to men's at-home wear. Eventually merging with Indian paisley motives, these dressing gowns supplanted the looser banyan and were a conflation of the various Easts. Here, they are worn with European pants, pumps, and gloves, as well as a cravat like that of the West, making the figure in Orientalist dress both an anomaly and strangely at home with his colleagues in the prevailing style of the United States and Europe.

Opposite page. Left: American. Man's lounging coat, late 1840s. Printed wool twill. Purchase, German Fur Industry Gift, 1981 (1981.12.4 a-c). Right: American. Man's smoking coat, 1860–80. Paisley-patterned wool. Gift of Anne L. Maxwell, 1989 (1989.246.2). In the tradition of the eighteenth-century banyan, nineteenth-century lounging robes and gowns alluded to their exotic sources. Paisley and Turkish motives were common and extended frequently to the decor of the smoking rooms to which men took their post-prandial retirement.

French. Tea gown, ca. 1891. Pieced panels of paisley-patterned woven wool shawl. Purchase, Irene Lewisohn and Alice L. Crowley Bequests, 1985 (1985.39.3). A tea gown is composed of a cut-up multicolored wool shawl woven in a Paisley pattern in imitation of a black-centered Indian Kashmir shawl. In fact, the material was probably woven in France during the 1860s or 1870s. On the upper right corner of the bodice is embroidered "Cachemire" in white thread. Such a tea gown, intended for gender-segregated leisure, is the feminine analogue to the man's dressing gown/smoking jacket.

Opposite page. Left: American. Coat, 1960s. Embroidered wool Kashmir shawl. Promised Gift of Mike Nevelson (L 1989.26.19). Right: Indian and French. Coat, 1959-63. Embroidered wool Kashmir shawl. Gift of Diana Vreeland, 1979 (1979.435.6). Kashmir shawls recut into coats indicate the persistence of the West's use of the shawl as an exotic basis for functional apparel. In the 1960s, India provided Western enthusiasts with a mystical attitude newly fueled by the cultures of music, hippie spiritualism, and drug-inflected idealism.

Alix Grès. Cocktail dress, ca. 1960. Magenta silk sari. Purchase, Gifts from various donors, 1993 (1993.190). Always sympathetic to the sari—its function to wrap and its propagation of bias as a consequence of spiraling drapery—Madame Grès was particularly influenced by her research sojourn in India in the 1950s. Grès's Orientalism has been comprehensive and continual: she was inspired by China and southeast Asia in the 1930s; she experimented later with dhoti and sari; she studied and sporadically used the caftans and loose drapery of North Africa and the Middle East; she simplified kimonos to her acutely reductive geometry in the 1960s.

Opposite page. Gianni Versace. Evening ensemble, spring-summer 1994. Purple, orange, and yellow crimped synthetic jersey. Courtesy Gianni Versace. With his tour-de-force fashion intelligence, Versace dissects and explodes the sari into separate color planes. The cropped yellow tee functions as a choli under a completely deconstructed sari that merges with punk via its safety-pin connectors and strident color. The diagonal one-shouldered top, a vestige of the sari's spiralling finish, has been transmogrified into Versace's sophisticated Milanese sensuality.

Near East and Middle East

The *Rubáiyát*'s poetry, as interpreted by Edward Fitzgerald, the foreign gallantry of Lord Byron, and the dreamer of Leigh Hunt: these are just a few among the legion of literary evocations, fixed in the nineteenth-century European mind, of an East of uncertain geographical location. North Africa and the Middle East were far less distant than the lands of the Far East. The crossing to them could be achieved readily, but their exotic charm could only be invoked by tales of enchantment. There would always be something wondrous about this place of imagination, filled with possibilities of lubricity, fascinating to Europe for its culture of multiple wives, subservient women, sexual license, and nomadic caravanserai. The hot and dry climate offered evasion of the cold and wet European and American winters, and it was so exotic to the European mind that it could only be perceived as a suite of places, never truly locatable. To be sure, the Orientalists were conversant with the facts and were even encouraged to think rationally about and travel to sites as worthy as the Holy Land, Egypt, and Persia, and the painters led the photographers to these destinations. Yet there were a thousand and one Orientalisms in the Near East and Middle East, each with, as Lynn

Opposite page and detail above. Mariano Fortuny. Dressing gown, 1920s. Stenciled rose silk. Gift of Mr. Courtlandt Palmer, 1950(CI 50.44). With slashed sleeves extending far beyond the length of arm like a mandarin's robes, Fortuny's wraps capes, and gowns are in the realm of high fantasy. Primary sign or reference—or what seems to be specific location—is established by the stenciling that suggests the Kufic and corded embroideries of North African djellabahs.

Thornton describes in *The Orientalists* (1978), "no particular regard for exactitude."

Thus, a Fortuny cape displays an evocative dislocation from the West, but its source is of no precise location in the East. Further, the Delphos or pleated gowns of Fortuny are mediated from the exotic through the classical, referencing the Western ancient world even more than the East. Venice, in its role as a crossroads and commercial city, but also as a place perpetuating carnivals, masquerades, and romance, provides a context for Fortuny's inventive appropriations from Eastern dress. The son of an artist who knew the conventions of an academic painter's artistic properties as they apply in dress and textiles, Fortuny became a fashion designer-inventor who called upon a stockpile of Eastern motives with regularity. He could allow a draped sleeve to suggest Ali Baba or a particular pattern to evoke North Africa, but seldom did he define the garment so that one can connect it to a specific time and place. Other Orientalists, particularly British artists, would see the East archaeologically and analytically, but Fortuny's Orient was as magical and as indefinite as Delacroix's, hovering between a pilgrim's specificity and a romantic's allure. As Barbara Baines has argued in *Fashion Revivals* (1981), even the

Above left. Formal gown à la sultane. *Galerie de la Mode*, 1782.
Above right. Court gown à la Turque. *Galerie de la Mode*, 1787. Left.
Costume of a Sultane. *Galerie de la Mode*, 1779. Manifestations of
the imagined Middle East vacillate between elements of theatrical accuracy and the adaptations required of more conventional dress.

Arab burnous entered the Eastern wardrobe as formal wrap in the middle of the nineteenth century, its capacious untailored shape capable of accommodating the great swells of crinolines under the skirt below it. Thus, the untailored Orientalist garment came to be popular in the West in part because the West did not have a comparably adaptable outer layer in accord with the inflated shape of 1860s fashion.

Of course, despite the fact that his allusions were supposedly historical, Fortuny was a fashion progressive and modernist. As Suzy Menkes has summarized in the *New York Times* (April 24, 1994) of ethnic fashion, "It has to be part of a modern landscape given just a touch of the exotic. Otherwise, the runway turns into a costume party or a perambulating tourist brochure." Fortuny avoided lapsing into mere costume or touristic garb by using the relaxed, untailored forms in accord with modern life. Earlier styles *à la turque* have often retained the silhouettes of Western dress, attempting to indicate signs of Turquerie with details such as aigrettes, stripes, and tassels—a strategy of limited application to dress. Fortuny's acumen was to perceive those elements that complement the modern and the Near Eastern that

Fashions of Paris, July 1799. In a splendid harmony, Ottoman and neoclassical references are fused in one garment. The hat is ambiguously depicted as a bonnet without its frame, bound by fabric knotted at its ends, in an allusion to a turban. The asymmetrical surplice neckline, fitted sleeves, long horsehoof cuffs, and tasseled sash are talismanic notes of an Ottoman presence within the prevailing Directoire silhouette.

A. Charles Jervas. *Lady Wortley-Montague in Turkish dress with a Clavicytherium*, ca. 1720. Oil on canvas. National Gallery of Ireland, Dublin. Brilliant diarist, letter-writer, and free thinker, Lady Wortley-Montague served in Constantinople with her ambassador-husband from 1717-1718. Her letters to Alexander Pope and other friends described with affection and analytical respect her times in Turkey.

Thomas Phillips. *Lord Byron*, 1814. Oil on canvas. National Portrait Gallery, London. Lord Byron in regional garb epitomized and even became an icon of the liberating power of the East, one that was in his case an imprecise sense of the Mediterranean around Greece. His depiction conveys a Hellenism tinged with the Ottoman; his portrait was intended to capture the spirit of the adventurer and agent of East to the West.

could make his garments more than souvenirs of tourism.

The masquerade that Menkes alludes to, with the assumption that it is inappropriate to modern life, was, of course, compelling in the eighteenth and nineteenth centuries. Thus, a comparison can be made between a Worth evening dress of about 1869 and a Ralph Lauren silk georgette ikat dress of spring 1994. Lauren seeks the redetermination of silhouette; his conceptual sensibility reaches far beyond concern with the textile pattern he has chosen to borrow. The Worth dress uses the East merely as a decorative overlay on the tiered silhouette that prevailed in Western fashion. If the East is to be a viable alternative, it most likely should involve fundamental change, not just superficial modification.

The nomadic life common in parts of the Middle East represented a particular option to the West, where growing urbanism was making it clear that the future would bring a lifestyle more settled and solidly passed in one place. A lingering wanderlust could convert gypsies into exotic queens, as in Henri Regnault's mid-nineteenth-century painting *Salomé*, which was very fashionable in its time. In a West that appeared to stifle the impulses to freedom more accessible in a less-industrialized East of very different customs, the appeal was to a sultry, earthy way of living that seemed the antipode of the social constraint of the "civilized" world in ascendancy. One cannot imagine the history of nineteenth-century art without the French paintings of women in Zouave jackets and ultimately, Van Gogh's representation of a man in Zouave trousers.

From Napoleon's sojourn in Egypt at the beginning of the nineteenth century until the Société des Peintres Orientalistes Français's creation in 1893 and the turn-of-the-century ardor for Byzantium—with European-sponsored archaeology and art history taking place in Istanbul, the Near East, and the Middle East—the landscape was changing continually from one of mystery and mirage to one of clear analytical discovery. By the time of T. E. Lawrence, there was a renewed desire for an alternative lifestyle in Islamic culture for the sophisticated Westerner. Intermittently, but never without interest since the birth of the modern period, the Orientalism of the Near East and Middle East was a persistent theme of the nineteenth century. Fauve painter Henri Matisse's kaleidoscopic and distilled Orientalism of the early twentieth century was still redolent of the long traditions of narrative incident and captivation. If there is any measure of a "returned gaze" in Western fashion, it is Yves Saint Laurent's brilliantly interpreted exoticisms. Saint Laurent, who was born in Morocco, has a strong affinity for Matisse, especially for the palette of the French painter's Moroccan figures and landscapes. Elsewhere, Saint Laurent is the virtuoso Orientalist—witness his "Russian" collection of fall-winter 1976-77, his Chinese-inspired fashions of fall-winter 1977-78, and his royal-India-related designs of fall-winter 1992.

English gentlemen of the nineteenth century

French. Mantle, 1870-75. White wool serge couched with metallic braid. Gift of Mrs. Philip K. Rhinelander, 1946 (46.25.4). American. Opera cloak, 1850s. Ivory silk faille embroidered with gold soutache braid. Gift of Mrs. Josephine Mingle Tennant, 1953 (CI 53.2). American (?). Dolman, ca. 1870. White silk poplin and braid. Gift of Mrs. George W. Heller, 1938 (CI 38.102). Mantle, cape, and dolman extend a relatively unstructured Eastern vocabulary to the Western tailored wardrobe. Couched gold braiding and fringed borders suggest North African dress in their palette and details. Similar scrolling embellishments are seen on the soutache-embroidered pique day dress à la Zouave in Monet's *Women in the Garden*.

might have espoused a taste for the classical, but it seems they preferred another perspective on the Mediterranean for their clothing, often wearing Turkish and North-African robes and other dress as signs of both opulence and leisure. Men smoking was a custom much associated with Turkey, Persia, and the rest of the leisurely-inhaling domain of North Africa. Western would-be sultans retired to smoking rooms after dinner to enjoy the social license of a men's society akin to that of the Arab world. They wore banyans and robes, informal attire that corresponded with Western un-dress. British statesman and author Benjamin Disraeli spoke of his pleasure in the "propriety and enjoyment" of a life modeled on that of the pashas, which allowed an English gentleman the luxury of smoking in repose. The connection went so far that a fez with tassel was sometimes worn by men in this supposedly salubrious, exotically-interpreted activity.

Turbans and bloomers came to the West with the sanction of the East. In the realm of headcoverings, adaptable for both men and women, the late-eighteenth- and early-nineteenth-century cult of the turban held little religious association; but it survived, often as a swirl of fabric wrapped around the more solid form generated from the hat block or more commonly a deflated puff of cloth eviscerated of any frame. Although the turban was transformed in the West, a semblance of the Eastern original was maintained by the addition of aigrettes and brooches. Bloomers, the controversial bifurcated garment advocated by Amelia Bloomer, were warranted in part by the East. Defenders offered the argument that Arab women had long worn a version of the garment without rising up to assume the prerogatives reserved for men and with an appropriately feminine gracefulness. In fact, Zouave trousers and pantaloons offered the primary visual evidence for and cultural recourse to the first arguments for women in pants. Eventually, pajamas would also

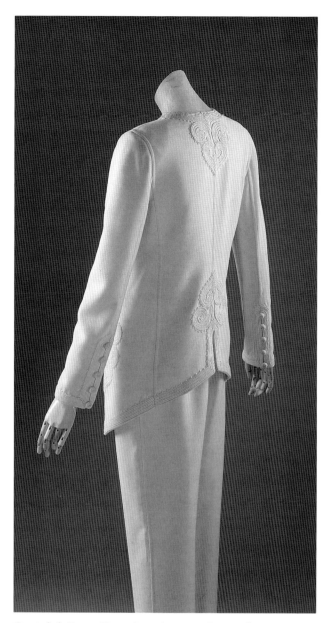

Oscar de la Renta. Day suit, spring 1994. Cream silk crepe. Courtesy Oscar de la Renta. De la Renta's eclecticism is never acquiescent. Instead, it is a critical clarification of exotic observations. Achieving elegance with his use of monochromatic cream, de la Renta relocates the traditional areas of embroidered ornament. The hem of the jacket that bifurcates obliquely alludes to the cut of Zouave uniforms. Risking the austere, this designer punctuates the jacket's severe cut with braid.

arrive, with a similar justification to an initially reluctant West.

The undifferentiated Mediterranean, Turkish, and Persian Easts became a land to be visited rather easily. Following the example of Delacroix, many European painters made chary journeys, preferring to fabricate whatever they had not noted or could not remember specifically. Fashion design benefited from the easy access to the areas' textiles and apparel. Barbara Baines cites commentary from *The Englishwoman's Domestic Magazine* (March 1867) on the market and its visibility, establishing a critical link to exhibitions and expositions of foreign goods, "This year's fashions seem to borrow something from the number of foreign costumes that are seen in Paris since the opening of the Great Exhibition. Amongst these the most eccentric are those that meet the most favour. Thus we have Chinese sleeves, Egyptian girdles, Turkish jackets, Russian touquets. It becomes more difficult than ever to dress really well and in good taste, and to avoid those fashions which are too much exaggerated to be ladylike." Indeed, the variety of exotic dress imported to the West was prodigious, but even more so was the West's desire to market and consume its own variations on Eastern attire.

Golden roads reportedly led to Samarkand, pilgrims' journeys led to the Holy Land, and colonists ventured to North Africa. But they all traveled with similar feelings of captivation with a Hajji Baba or Sardanapalus more opulent and more salubrious than any who dwelled only in the West. As Linda Nochlin has argued, the imagined East is an invention of Western deficiencies and desires. It is a perfect land, so proved because no traveler ever quite arrived there, yet every journey resulted in a bounty of treasured textiles and apparel.

Todd Oldham. Genie cut-out dress, 1991. Black wool embroidered with gold braid and plastic stones. Courtesy Todd Oldham. Oldham displaces with postmodern abandon. He does not seek a fictional Orientalism but rather, a quirky and media-inspired pastiche of Casbah and "I Dream of Jeannie." Oldham's portraits of bared abdomen and ribs employ an avant-garde strategy: an advanced fashion position is created in the ambiguous mix of an East that is knowingly misinterpreted and a West that permits the invention Oldham poses through its own history of distortion.

Opposite page. Left: French. Dress, ca. 1755. Chiné-patterned silk taffeta. Gift of Fédération de la Soirie, 1950 (50.168.1 a,b). Right: French. Robe à la Polonaise (open robe and matching petticoat), last quarter 18th century. Chiné-patterned silk taffeta.(L 39.29.1 a,b). Rococo style embraced foreign styles with an inclusive, even rapacious eclecticism, but also with its own propensity to moderation and the small scale. During the period, ikat, or warp-printed fabric, was modified to meet European taste. Saturated Eastern colors and bold geometrics became muted pastels in smaller floral and striped patterns characterizing many of the designs.

Ralph Lauren. Dress, spring 1994. Ikat-patterned silk georgette. Courtesy Ralph Lauren. In contrast to eighteenth-century European ikats, Lauren's designs, while printed rather than woven, are faithful to the scale and palette of Asian ikats, though the dress and pattern become a conscious fusion of several Easts, including Southeast Asia and China. In the 1990s, the emerging economic and social power of Southeast Asia, renewed after years of conflict and war, holds a romantic impact for the West, especially evident in such movies as *The Lover* (from the Marguerite Duras novella) and *Indochine*.

Opposite page. Charles Frederick Worth. Evening dress, ca. 1872. Peacock-blue silk faille with trim of ivory silk satin embroidered with silk floss and cream silk tulle. Gift of Mrs. Philip K. Rhinelander, 1946 (46.25.1 a-d). Worth seldom scrutinized the East or assimilated from it. More often he was the instrument of a Western taste that was projected onto imperialism. He is said to have created 250 dresses on commission from the Empress Eugénie for her appearances at the opening of the Suez Canal in 1868. In this rare case, Worth emulates Middle Eastern enamels. Nonetheless, he was known for his fancy-dress costumes of the period that cited Eastern origins mediated through the European perspectives of the Renaissance, Tudor England, or Venice.

Henri Regnault. *Salomé*, 1869-70. Oil on canvas. Gift of George F. Baker, 1916 (16.95). Hybrid exoticism, mixing Italy with the Near East, became a convention of nineteenth-century representation. Adding to the intermingling of locales at mid-century, there was a new icon: the ennobled and voluptuous peasant who knows no specific place but suggests universal origins. Rustic longings, sublimated eroticism, and languorous exoticism animate this painting, ostensibly of narrative subject but perhaps addressed more directly to the ineffable yearnings that characterized the period.

Maurice Babani. Dress, ca. 1925. Yellow silk velvet couched with gold braid. Gift of Mrs. Aline Bernstein, 1945 (CI 45.91.2). Babani's garments were, in general, more literal in their relationship to sources than Fortuny's. This dress is specifically derived from North African apparel, though here Babani uses silk velvet instead of the wool characteristic of his North African sources.

Opposite page: Mariano Fortuny. Evening cape, early 1930s. Mauve-and-gray striped silk velvet. Gift of C. J. Vincent Minetti, 1972 (1972.209.28). Fortuny's artist-father created with access to an aficionado's collection of diverse historicist and exotic objects. He collected North-African textiles and costume and used them as studio props. The younger Fortuny continued the life of such objects in what he characterized as his inventions, a science applied to dress. This evening wrap is almost literally a berber cape, except for the specific textile (silk velvet) and embellishments (metallic stenciling) typical of Fortuny.

Opposite page. American. Evening dress, 1923. Black silk satin woven with silver thread with velvet-and-mink trim. Gift of Mrs. Morton E. Snellenburg, 1946 (CI 46.46.2). This American dress, featured in *Theater Magazine* (November 1922), is based on an original model by Poiret. It demonstrates the dissemination of Poiret's theatrically intense Bakst- and Ballet-Russes-inspired Orientalism, a salient trait of Poiret's.

Paul Poiret. Day dress, 1921. Black silk crepe and deep red silk satin brocaded with gold. Gift of Leone B. Moats, in memory of Mrs. Wallace Payne Moats, 1979 (1979.428). The Turkish mode of the 1920s had a few simple style-signs, each an inflected version of one of the signifiers of the modern in dress. A barely-fitted bodice, dipping waist, and flared skirt, while orientalizing in effect, conform to the reigning silhouette of the day.

Callot Soeurs. Day dress, ca. 1924. Woven cashmere embroidered with gold thread. Gift of Julia B. Henry, 1978 (1978.288.7 a,b). Referencing Persia, the Callot Soeurs create a kind of artistic dress of the 1920s, stark in tubular silhouette but ornamented as surface. Despite the presence of decoration, for which they were perhaps best known at the time, the Callot Soeurs practiced a disciplined modernism. The day dress with collarless tunic employs a vestigially Ottoman, angled sleeve with narrow cuffs.

Opposite page. Left: Callot Soeurs. Evening dress, ca. 1925. Silk floss embroidered green silk crepe. Gift of Isabel Shults, 1944 (CI 44.64.12). Right: Callot Soeurs. Evening dress, ca. 1925. Silk floss embroidered magenta silk crepe. Gift of Isabel Shults, 1944 (CI 44.64.13 a-c). Dresses by Callot Soeurs feature long fluid versions of the vestigial sleeves seen on Ottoman coats. The Callots are more widely known for their Chinoiserie, but their Persian-Turkish styles often share the same sense of Chinese color.

Opposite page. Left: Jessie Franklin Turner. Dress, ca. 1926. Gray silk crepe brocaded with gold thread. Gift of Mrs. Aline Bernstein, 1945 (CI 45.103.1). Right: Jeanne Lanvin. Afternoon dress, ca. 1927. Cream silk satin embroidered with multicolored silk floss and silver thread. Gift of Natica Nast Warburg, 1978 (1978.127.2). Established in small-scale patterns, the Orientalist frame of reference is extended by the designers' use of the gored panels and braid-edge closures of Ottoman clothing. Both of the dresses were owned by women of independent, artistic style: the allure of Turquerie was a tonic, a kind of sophisticated aesthetic dress appealing especially to powerful women in the arts.

Maggy Rouff. Evening coat, ca. 1934. Light blue and metallic gold brocaded white silk with ermine trim. Gift of Mrs. Maxime L. Hermanos, 1959 (CI 59.37.1). The hieratic, almost two-dimensional cuts of Turkish robes are alluded to but modified by Rouff in her evening coat. Of course, the ceremonial style of the Turkish court can also be explained by the contemporary vogue for a softened A-line skirt. Modernism's unremitting progress in the 1920s and 1930s could seem mitigated and justified by the collateral referencing to the Turkish style.

Opposite page. Rifat Ozbek. Evening ensemble, 1994. Gray satin with fur trim and pink silk taffeta. Courtesy Rifat Ozbek. Ozbek creates a dramatic, bandstand Turquerie. The narrow top is based on a Turkish military overvest, and the bubble skirt evokes the ballooning legs of Zouave pants. By the 1990s, some inhibitions haunt such hyperbolic Orientalism, associated by some with the politics of imperialism. Ozbek, born in Turkey and living in England, accepts the possibilities and interpretive challenge of an overt exoticism without the onus of political judgment.

Romeo Gigli. Tunic ensemble, spring/summer 1990. Metallic gauze with Venetian-glass. Courtesy Romeo Gigli. Gigli's Orientalism is a bricolage of his studied interest in the East, his personal and literary travels, and his sense of the ethereal femininity often projected on women outside the West. His evocation is more like an early-twentieth-century Scheherazade than an authentic or ethnographic view. Using Venetian glass, Gigli constructs a fragility whose objectification of an illusory feminine ideal has long been an Orientalist fantasy.

Japan

After 250 years of isolation, Japan burst open, to the immediate joy and edification of the West. In 1862, E. Desoye opened a shop of Japanese curios at 220, rue de Rivoli, Paris. In 1875, Arthur Lasenby Liberty was selling the new and exotic-style works of art and fabric on Regent Street in London. The craze for things Japanese was anchored in England, America, and France, where there was a supreme sense of respect for Japanese ritual and etiquette and a profusion of fabric and woodblock prints of swathed figures moving in ideal space. In the 1880s—confirmed in posters advertising it by Toulouse-Lautrec—one of the chicest cabarets in Paris was the Divan Japonais, a place where fans and silks festooned the walls and patrons were served by waitresses dressed in kimono. Even deportment and how it was depicted seemed to change under the influence of Japan. The isolationism of Japan in the Shogunate period had definitely ended. Japan did not seep gently into Europe as other Orientalisms had; it arrived as an aesthetic and cultural tsunami. Japonisme was a mercantile fast-boat that carried impressions and artifacts in plenitude with many of the objects providing accurate renderings illustrating the land so long an enigma to the West.

Opposite page and detail above. Jeanne Lanvin. Evening ensemble, ca. 1934. Black silk taffeta with metal plaques. Gift of Miriam W. Coletti, 1993 (1993.423.1 a,b). Lanvin's evening bolero resembles the tubular construction of the kimono and its sleeves. However, Lanvin modifies her simulation by radically cropping the kimono's parts. The three-diamond shape (the diamonds are superimposed on one another) composed of metal plaques is an allusion to the *mon*, a Japanese clan insignia. The plaques were more commonly used on Egyptian *irsuit* shawls, a popular historicism-exoticism of the same period.

Even before the Meiji era began in 1868, Japan's precipitous opening in 1854 to Western eyes and trade had begun to alter the Western world. Japan's isolation had been deliberate and definitive; it had sought to avoid the promulgations of missionaries.

Japan's seclusion had been long; when Admiral Perry's "black ships" were permitted to land in Yokohama, the West was ready to embrace the culture it did not know. Perhaps the West was even ready to replace the culture that it did know, its own.

Moreover, Japan and the West were immediately served by two-way traffic; the island nation was as voraciously interested in the West as the West was desirous of Japanese styles. Meiji Japan was an era of transformation that reflected Western modernity, and an equally intense eagerness in the West changed modern art and culture. Adding to the complications, Japan afforded the West both the brazen and vivid cultures of Samurai, Kabuki, and Yoshiwara, and the contemplative, reflective ideals of Zen, tea ceremony and codes of deference. There are many Japans in the Western imagination.

The West's ebullient enthusiasm for Japan is unlike that of any other Orientalism. More impas-

Hashimoto Chikanobu. *A Group of Children Playing Under the Plum Blossoms in the Snow*, 1887. Woodblock print. The Metropolitan Museum of Art, Gift of Lincoln Kirstein, 1959 (JP3341). Japan's traffic with the West was energetic in both directions. Western traditions and needs merged with Japanese manufacture under Emperor Meiji's directive to Japan to participate in the wider economic world.

sioned than its embrace of the Near East, more comprehending than its knowledge of China, and more engaged than with Kiplingesque India, the decisive Japonisme of the nineteenth and twentieth centuries created philosophical and cultural involvements with Zen spiritualism, haiku reductivism, Kabuki grandiloquence, and a pantheistic communion with nature that Frank Lloyd Wright, among many other artists and thinkers, saw so clearly and paradigmatically as Japanese. Japan is not a monolithic Orientalism of a single expression: while its cultural complexity has seldom been seen in its entirety, it has been understood for its variety. Cherry blossom, pictographic script, and rising sun are signs with a panoply of symbolic extensions.

In fact, the West customarily has seen a Japan of blatant and showy *hade* values as well as a Japan of serene *jimi* quietude. The paradox for the West has always been the coexistence of warrior violence and harakiri with gentle aestheticism, of Edo and the Floating World with Kyoto and moss gardens of serenity, and of Kabuki's extravagance with the cryptic stylizations of Noh. The terseness of tatami

space could seem to contradict the expansiveness of Japanese culture. Even clothing covered a spectrum from flamboyant theatrical dress to the hermetic, ritual kimono. Emile Zola was represented by Édouard Manet as an Occidental contemplative who emulates and commands Japanese aesthetics, and conversely, Toulouse-Lautrec was photographed decked out in Japanese travesty as demonstratively and ostentatiously as possible.

To the West, Japan is both picturesque and the avatar of modernist principles. The representations on early examples of Ukiyoe prints imported from Japan showed the West the customary, if fairyland, character of Japanese daily life. Lanvin's dress with bolero jacket of about 1934, which simulates kimono sleeves, has a perspective on Japanese sensibility distilled by Western modernity. The interlocking plates that are the sole ornamentation are a design minimalism that show Lanvin moving toward one of her more modernist efforts.

The West never sought to emulate the complicated wrapped closure of the kimono's obi but instead coopted its principle of a flattened form surrounding the body. The coexistence of kimono and bias in 1920s and 1930s fashion was not entirely a historical accident. Both forms of draping—the first enveloping and the other disclosing and emphasizing—circulate around the body cylindrically, breaking zones of front and back, establishing clothing as a gyrating cylinder surrounding the wearer. This concept, fundamentally aligned with if not specifically occasioned by Cubism's elementary cylinders, obtained both in the foreign magic of Japanese design and in the formalism of Western evolution to basic structure. Julia Meech and Gabriel P. Weisberg conclude their book, *Japonisme Comes to America* (1990), with the acknowledgment that "Japonisme reinforced the romantic ideals of numerous artists at the turn of the century. For others it served as a catalyst in the exploration of modernist aesthetics. Such was and is today Japan's ironic enticement to the West."

Often, of course, this "coincidence" or cultural correspondence between Japanese aesthetics and modernist strivings gives rise to ambiguity. In the McCardell silk evening dress, the reference to Japanese dress could almost be overlooked, so consonant is this garment with McCardell's design development. Further, McCardell's resemblance in this instance to Fortuny or Grès provides an imbroglio of possible sources.

Bernard Rudofsky's ingenious text, *The Kimono Mind* (1965), attempts to understand Japan through the metaphor of the kimono, acknowledging in a quote from Lafcadio Hearn that the Westerner must "feel indescribably toward Japan." Rudofsky is perspicacious in thinking of apparel as a significant form of expression and even as a mediation between Japan and the West. He reports that the Japanese would often ask of visitors from the West if they liked the kimono, seeking Western approval of the form of dress as the central metaphor for cultural approval. In fact, the "kimono mind" even transcends the era of the kimono and may stand in some way as an abiding metaphor for Japan. Thus, recent fashion from Japan that supplants the kimono but prizes its principles of wrapping and textile unity has

had a profound effect on contemporary dress. In the Philadelphia Museum of Art catalog *Japanese Design: A Survey Since 1950* (1994), Akiko Fukai assesses in her essay on fashion, "Simply, these [Japanese] designers dismantled the symbolism that had become ingrained in Western clothing during the nineteenth century. If Japanese fashion revolutionized the international fashion scene, and it continues to do so, this is not just an indication of Japan's originality; it may be a proposal for a clothing of the future that will transcend ethnic and gender differences and even the confines of an establishment called fashion." The testimony to the most recent influence of Japanese fashion in the West only affirms the continued impact of Japanese apparel since the Meiji period.

As Fukai argues, gender and ethnicity play a role

Édouard Manet. *Portrait of Zola*, 1868. Oil on canvas. Musée du Louvre, Paris. In the 1860s, the literary and cultural intelligentsia was keenly aware of Japan and enthralled by its objects and methods of visualization. In portraying Zola's intellectual world as an aficionado of things Japanese, Manet also projects his own interest in the prints, their compositional devices, and their preoccupation with a passing world.

in the inspiration that contemporary Japanese fashion affords the West. The discernible difference—to the West's unaccustomed eyes seldom differentiated—between men's and women's apparel promotes Japan's preference for a dress that discounts gender differentiation, deviating from the Western principle of associating dress with sexual allure. The perceived disassociation between clothing and sexual allure that occurs in Japanese dress affords a significant option to Western dress, with its strong reliance on body expression and sexuality in women's clothing. Further, ethnicity is also suppressed in the amalgams of Chinese, Japanese, Indian, and Southeast Asian dress that come to the Western imagination. Unable to see specific ethnic origins, the West permits the aura and does not require a specific anthropological place. Hybrid styles by such designers as Hanae Mori and Issey Miyake offer the paradigm of dress that cannot be located to a specific place but that justly belong to the world. The calligraphy of the Hanae Mori gowns, for example, is probably unintelligible to most in the West. And the specific sources of Ronaldus Shamask's *hakama*-pants outfits need not be traced to Japan: their utility and ingenuity speak for themselves.

In the 1870s, Japanese courtiers and government

Alfred Stevens. *In the Studio*, 1888. Oil on canvas. Gift of Mrs. Charles Wrightsman, 1986 (1986.339.2). By the final years of the nineteenth century Orientalism was the most important aesthetic discourse, challenging minds and talents as diverse as Stevens, Ernest Fenollosa, Whistler, Van Gogh, and Tissot. In his depiction of the artist's studio, Stevens scatters the props of Japonisme—a fan, a paper parasol, and, most notably in a conflation of the Easts, the model's Chinese robe.

Henri de Toulouse Lautrec, ca. 1892. Photograph: Musée Toulouse-Lautrec-Albi-Tam-France. Kimono, hat, fan, and doll suggest Toulouse-Lautrec's literal embodiment of a Japanese world. His art represents the same enthusiasm for the principles of Japanese art, especially its communicative forms as reflected in printmaking and posters. Inevitably, the image suggests both fanatical enthusiasm and a peculiar naiveté, both of which may be parts of late-nineteenth-century aesthetic imperialism.

officials on duty with Western nations were expected to wear Western dress. In response, the English Japanophile Arthur Diosy rallied with a spirited defense of Japanese dress, extolling the kimono as "simple in cut, sombre in colour, neat to a degree, and excellent in taste." The argument for simplicity was buttressed by Diosy's approval of Japanese clothing for hygiene and comfort better attuned than Western dress to the climate of Japan.

One hundred years later, the West began to respond to a contemporary Japanese ethos of dress introduced by Issey Miyake and later by Rei Kawakubo for Comme des Garcons. Roles were reversed when fashion of the 1970s and 1980s was increasingly shaped by Japanese-born designers of an international spirit such as these two. The most modern in fashion was being generated once again out of the steadfast principles of traditional Japanese design.

Opposite page. Left: Japanese for Western market. Dressing gown, ca. 1880. Quilted blue silk. Gift of Katherine Babcock Cavalli, 1970 (1970.83 a,b). Right: Japanese for Western market. Dressing gown, late 1880s. Quilted brown silk. Gift of Theodore Fischer Ells, 1975 (1975.227.7 a,b). In the nineteenth century Japan produced prodigiously for its new Western market. Economic initiative caused the Japanese to create consumer items exclusively for the export market. At the same time, Japan began massive consumption of Western goods, chiefly in the sectors of heavy industry and engineering. Quilted dressing gowns like these two are for an occasion and of a style that would never have been operative in Japan. For the European customer, the pattern of late-spring flowers, insects, and lotuses was evocative of the exotic origins that are mitigated by the accommodations to Western style. Like James Abbott McNeill Whistler and the French Impressionists, fashion embraced Japonisme with alacrity.

Iida and Company / Takashimaya. Theater coat, ca. 1900. Ivory silk embroidered with gray and black silk floss. Gift of Joseph L. Brotherton, 1985 (1985.362.1). The kimono and the bamboo pattern are principal signifiers of Japan in the West. The adaptation of a theater coat from the silhouette of the kimono accommodates styles and needs of the Western market but also retains close identification with Japanese sources. By 1900 exoticism was customarily accompanied by reductivism, accepting and exacerbating the potential of Asian dress for modernism. This theater coat was published in the January–March 1900 issue of the fashion magazine *The Delineator*.

Gabrielle ("Coco") Chanel. Theater coat, ca. 1927. Black and white gold-brocaded silk crepe. Purchase, Irene Lewisohn Bequest; Catherine Breyer Von Bomel Foundation Fund; Hoechst Fiber Industries Fund; Chauncey Stillman Fund, 1984 (1984.30). The convergence of Art Déco line, the modernist impulse to facilitate pure form, and Japonisme's potential to offer a vocabulary of untailored wrapping shapes was more than fortuitous. Chanel uses a French ombréed textile with pattern sources from the Japanese kimono but brings to it the ethos of chaste minimalism. As fashion realized from the East that untailored lengths of fabric could constitute modern dress, the cylinder and textile plane became the new forms for apparel. Japan's role is a chicken-and-egg conundrum: did Japan provide the cause and model or merely a correlated example?

Cristobal Balenciaga. Evening wrap, 1954-55. Red-pink silk faille. Gift of Baroness Philippe de Rothschild, 1973 (1973.21.3). Conversant with Spanish ceremonial and vernacular dress as an expression of European regionalism, Balenciaga likewise respected Orientalism as a source to be modified in modern apparel. In one wrap, he refers to two Orientalist effects. The cocoon shape of the back alludes to the way a Japanese woman's outer kimono accommodates over her obi to create an elegant arc. More evidently, in emphasizing the nape of the neck by dropping the bias-rolled collar, he evokes the kimono's band neckline, which dips at back. Balenciaga's objective may have been a soft attenuation of the neck in the manner of Ingres's swanlike extension of anatomy, but he also recognized the kimono as his paradigm.

Claire McCardell. Evening dress, 1950. Red silk damask. Gift of Irving Drought Harris, in memory of Claire McCardell Harris, 1958 (CI 58.49.4 a,b). McCardell's enthusiasm and acumen for European fashion history is well documented, but her interests extended East as well. This evening dress suggests Chinese roots in its textile, pleating, and color, but it also evokes Japanese origins in its wide sash (like an obi) and columnar silhouette. In a global eclecticism, the dress is cut like a poncho with its top crisscrossed over the bodice to create the kimono-like surplice neckline.

Opposite page. Thea Porter. Caftan, ca. 1969. Orange silk. Courtesy Eleanor Lambert. In the 1960s, a naive and jet-abetted hippie quest was to find world peace and knowledge. The clothing of the period combined disparate styles, particularly those that seemed native or genuinely rustic. Thus, Porter employs a caftan with details of its North African source, but she merges that imagery with a wide obi-like sash that cinches in the waist and creates drapery at the sides in the effect of a kimono's *nagasode* (long pendant sleeves).

Opposite page. Left: Hanae Mori. Calligraphy gown, 1989. Black-patterned white silk chiffon. Courtesy Hanae Mori. Right: Hanae Mori. Calligraphy gown, 1989. White patterned black silk chiffon. Courtesy Hanae Mori. As the first Japanese fashion designer to achieve international standing, beginning with her premier New York showing in January 1965, Mori has consistently merged the principles of Japanese aesthetics with the traditions of haute couture. The Japanese calligraphy with wide, sumi-painting brushstrokes on chiffon and a faint retention of the obi in the narrow satin sashes on these gowns are tokens of Japan.

Left: Valentino. Cocktail suit, fall–winter 1987–88. Yellow, black, and white sequined black silk crepe with black silk velvet. Courtesy Valentino. Right: Valentino. Cocktail ensemble, fall–winter 1987–88. Gold and black sequined black silk with black silk organza. Courtesy Valentino. The decoration of sequin and bead embroidery does not refer to Japanese dress but instead to gilded black lacquer boxes of the Japanese decorative arts. The fact that S. Bing's primary intervention on behalf of Japonisme was a decorative arts shop suggests the prevalence of this repertoire of objects, which serve as easy signs of the Japanese taste just as much as wisteria, pagoda, or bamboo patterns do.

Opposite page. Left: Ronaldus Shamask. *Hakama* ensemble, 1979. Red silk taffeta. Courtesy Ronaldus Shamask. Right: Ronaldus Shamask. *Hakama* overalls, 1979. Black silk taffeta. Courtesy Ronaldus Shamask. Shamask offers a contemporary Japanese sensibility replete with the knowing enthusiasm of traditional American Japanophiles such as Fenollosa and Dow. But he seeks modified, interpreted forms. For example, his versions of formal Japanese menswear (*hakama*, or full bifurcated skirt) imply a gender switch to womenswear. With changed proportions and the shifting of the waist to the neckline, they become evening dresses. In the red ensemble, *hakama* are paired with an origami top of elaborately folded sleeves, another Western cipher for a Japanese sensibility.

Issey Miyake. Dress, 1989. Gray and black pleated polyester. Courtesy Emilie de Brigard. Futuristic in visual impression and sensibility, Miyake's dress also acknowledges tradition. It resembles a man's formal over-kimono with extended shoulders. Short sleeves project outward as if from an under-kimono. In fact, Miyake has made one garment. Unlike the symmetry of the formal man's kimono, the effect is created by the asymmetrical placement of color blocks and sleeve elements. Miyake's critical enterprise is always to harmonize the history of Eastern and Western apparel with avant-garde apparel.

Southeast Asia

The Siamese Embassy to Versailles and the Court of Louis XIV in 1686 provoked a frenzy of Orientalist design. But it was the habit of the West to combine and generalize the various Easts, and the new decorative style, even the narrative components of its imagery, was merged into a monolithic Chinoiserie. For centuries, the distinctions of the various kingdoms of Southeast Asia were blurred in the popular Western imagination with those of their Chinese and Indian neighbors. It is only recently, with the final dissolution of Western colonial authority in the region, that it has come to be differentiated as a distinctive East.

In many ways, therefore, Southeast Asia is the newest among the venerable Easts. Situated along the trade routes between China and Europe, Southeast Asia has an image that is compelling in the eyes of Western novelists such as Somerset Maugham or Marguerite Duras. It even reaches the realm of the fantastic in the conjury of *Anna and the King of Siam* and its later form, *The King and I*, in which the American world of *Uncle Tom's Cabin* and the dancing world of colonialism are transposed.

Over the centuries, portals to the East have opened and closed. The rueful departure of the French from Indo-China temporarily closed a door. More decisively, the War in Vietnam and its permeation into Laos and Cambodia stifled the possibility for American and European visions of those lands to be nurtured and grow. A mere twenty years after the war and its attendant bitter defeats raged across those territories, Southeast Asia has been replenished, and it now holds the promise of a brighter future. Battlefields of the recent past have become domains of fashion ideals. Is apparel the pacifier, or is it merely the most accommodating of cultural forms?

In fact, apparel can be an appeasement of history and geography precisely because of clothing's significance and capacity to act as a nonverbal mediator. Without having to announce peace, defeat, or victory, clothing functions as a means of recognizing common traits. The cheongsam with its long asymmetrical wrap that is seen in Southeast Asia is a historical transplant from China; it has stimulated the imagination of designers. Film has helped alert Western fashion to the rich possibilities of Southeastern dress. The films *The Lover* and *Indochine*, for example, have served to romanticize the apparel of Vietnam, emphasizing its modernity and adaptability.

Opposite page and detail above. Oscar de la Renta. Evening sarong ensemble, fall–winter 1990–91. Maroon velvet with glass-beaded silk satin. Courtesy Oscar de la Renta. The sarong is one of the most evocative garments of the Asian vocabulary in the twentieth century, suggesting an idyllic, feminine, Polynesian beauty and clothing for leisure. Dorothy Lamour movies and the sarong's improvisational aspect suggest an exotic informality and casual sensuality. Throughout his career de la Renta has sought to distill from the East the ingenious cuts and extravagant ornament of its dress.

Reflecting on recent signs of global ethnicity in dress earlier this year, Suzy Menkes reported in the *New York Times* (April 24, 1994), "Ethnic clothes in the modern age are not just about re-creating the patterns of India at the time of the moguls or the brocades of China's last emperor. The simple woven cottons that were once peasant clothing are also a strong trend. Issey Miyake's fabric research includes not just space-age pleated materials, but also re-creations of the thick padded cottons and natural dyes inspired by traditional Japanese fisherman's clothing. Paradoxically, these once humble materials are now highly priced because the time and skills of hand labor that were once taken for granted are now luxuries." Menkes's notice that contemporary fashion designers are observing peasant traditions and vernacular dress as much as court costume is particularly apt in this case. After all, the ikat and khaki renderings of the cheongsam made in Southeast Asia and brought to the West are based on the attire of ordinary people. The elegance attributed to the cheongsam in the West is as willful an inversion as the little black dress of Chanel is, although in the case of the cheongsam, the material ascends rather than descends. In the quest for a fashion that may surpass a tradition of elite origins and trickle-down style, Eastern dress poses an alternative. We in the West relinquish only reluctantly our ancien régime of the couture's hegemony and of fashion's status. In its decision to abandon a long-standing model of a sumptuary art emanating from and aspiring to high style and rarity of materials—a significant cultural determination—the West has prized the alternative of the East. It is ironic that lands of dominion have provided paradigms that displace traditional Western social hierarchy, and the distinction of much non-Western fashion admired in the West in the late years of the twentieth century has been that it is clothing for the regular people. Indeed, in modern times the political displacements prevalent in previously conquered lands may suggest a new political and social order that is represented by the fact that clothing of the people has become highly prized.

Inevitably, Orientalism in the West has always combined dreams of the exotic and dominion over it.

The empires that arrogantly sought partners for exchange and/or exploitation, that desired colonies to assure the cooperation of subject peoples, and that plundered economies and rendered colonial cultures dependent on the West, are the concomitants of the West's dreaming vision of a perfect East. Like any other source of Edenic innocence, the East was despoiled almost as readily as it was desired. As an English writer described with implacable melancholy, it was perceived of as the "lost horizon." The British, French, Dutch, and American authority that once held sway in Southeast Asia is not forgotten, yet the West has returned to Southeast Asia with new eyes and new interest. Edward Said, in *Culture and Imperialism* (1993), finds a brave post-colonialism in the Romanesque mind of Hugo of St. Victor, whom Said quotes, " 'The person who finds his homeland sweet is still a tender beginner; he to whom every soil is as his native one is already strong; but he is perfect to whom the entire world is a foreign place. The tender soul has fixed his love on one spot in the world; the strong person has extended his love to all places; the perfect man has extinguished his.' "

As a cultural art, fashion is not entirely blameless for the imperialism that surrounds much of the extension of European curiosity and commerce into faraway places. Textiles and fashion are an overt form of commerce. Nonetheless, fashion's acquisitive view of the world is only partly about possession and possessions. Additionally, fashion quests for design ideas, new materials, and a refreshment in the universal exercise of adorning the body and articulating individual and cultural needs through apparel. The successive voyages East sought much in mind, in politics, and in chattel. Apparel stimulated possibilities, advanced colonial politics, and rendered goods. Orientalism in Western fashion is, however, also an unquenchable dream and an unending, ever-optimistic journey.

Yves Saint Laurent. Pagoda ensemble, spring–summer 1980. Gilt embroidered black silk gazar. Gift of Diana Vreeland, 1984 (1984.607.28a,b,c). Marguerite Duras wrote in appreciation of Saint Laurent's synthesizing imagination, "I tend to believe that the fabulous universality of Yves Saint Laurent comes from a religious disposition toward garnering the real, be it man-made—the temples of the Nile—or not man-made—the forest of Telemark, the floor of the ocean, or apple trees in bloom. Yves Saint Laurent invents a reality and adds it to the other, the one he has not made." In this case, Saint Laurent invents a mysterious East and adds it to the Stendhalian valor of formal military dress.

Opposite page. Left: Ralph Lauren.
Ensemble, spring–summer 1994.
Paisley-patterned cocoa silk georgette
with khaki washed-silk taffeta.
Courtesy Ralph Lauren. Right: Ralph
Lauren. Ensemble, spring 1994.
Paisley-patterned silk georgette with
khaki washed-silk taffeta. Courtesy
Ralph Lauren. Lauren pacifies
Indochina in the mood of the 1990s.
Acclaiming the Vietnamese peasant
costume, Lauren brings to Southeast
Asia the same historically redolent,
enhanced past that he is known for
ascribing to the American West,
establishment and sporting America,
and the United Kingdom. Long
tunics over tight-fitting pants were
originally introduced to Southeast
Asia under the influence of Chinese
costume. Like Somerset Maugham,
Lauren appreciates but burnishes the
traditions—in this case, batik-
inspired patterns in soft European
textiles.

Ralph Lauren. Evening ensemble,
spring-summer 1994. Beaded indigo
silk chiffon. Courtesy Ralph Lauren.
The high neckline and traditional
regional wrapping with an asym-
metrically tied waist wrap or stole are
allusions to Southeast-Asian dress.
Lauren works in indigo, a fabric dye
characteristic of regional rural dress,
but he embellishes the design with
luxurious beading. The contrasting
juxtaposition of peasant-dress color
with opulent beading results in a
dress that is, paradoxically, both simple and sumptuous.

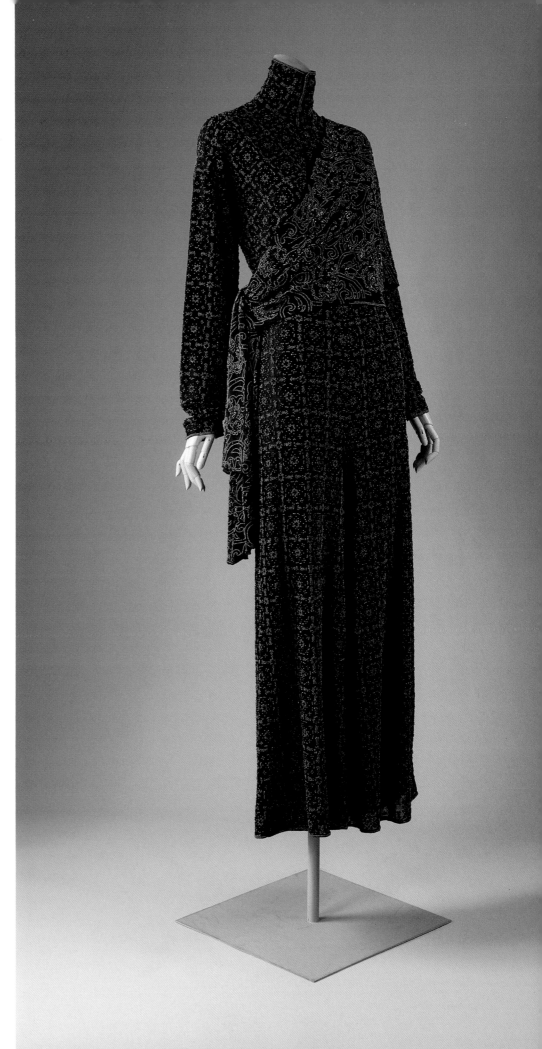

Acknowledgments

"There is," said nineteenth-century American writer Herman Melville, "some sort of Cape Horn for all." That even a preliminary account of Orientalism in fashion has not heretofore been offered either in exhibition or in book form suggests that our enterprise was, if not foolhardy, at least adventuresome. Without doubts, parts of this story have been told. Most recently, the investigations of our friends Akiko Fukai and Jun Kanai for the Kyoto Costume Institute's 1994 exhibition *Japonism in Fashion* have charted a part of the domain we have chosen to study. The breadth and the intensity of the Western wardrobe's assimilation of the East are readily seen in the collection of The Costume Institute. Not a single donor to The Costume Institute was preoccupied with our subject, yet throughout the collection, examples abound, including many more than could be presented in one exhibition.

We offer thus a prospectus and a polemic more than a finished enterprise on Orientalism in dress. It is important to see the "big picture" involving many colonial powers, countless traders and voyages, and many lands both on the map and in the mind and to realize the mesmerizing and recurrent impact of the Orient on the Western fashion imagination. Further, we wanted not to exculpate fashion from colonialism and commerce but to appreciate the way fashion works on an aesthetic basis. Thus, our task here is finite and preparatory; much study remains to be done. There is much to see and know. At the same time, there is all the hope of the East that is yet to be prized.

We are grateful to many individuals who have generously helped with this small book and exhibition. In particular, we have been inspired by the beautiful photographs of Karin Willis, assisted by Judith Perkins. Her respectful and careful reading of apparel combines with her sensibility for the vivacious photograph. Similarly, these photographs benefit from the clever and lyrical mannequin dressing of Joell Kunath. We have avoided static-doll imperialism through the fresh visions imparted to clothing by Karin and Joell.

We are grateful for the kindnesses and cooperation of: Iris Barrel Apfel, Attata Foundation; Arlene C. Cooper; Emilie de Brigard; Titi Halle and Donna Ghelerter, Cora Ginsburg; Martin Kamer; Mrs. Thomas Kempner; Eleanor Lambert; Muriel Kallis Steinberg Newman; Kevin Stayton and Patricia Mears, The Brooklyn Museum; Melissa Leventon, The Fine Arts Museums of San Francisco; Akiko Fukai and Jun Kanai, Kyoto Costume Institute; Linda Gaunt and Cindy Sirko, Giorgio Armani; Justo Artigas, Dolce e Gabbana; Itsuko Kaneda and Natasha, Romeo Gigli; Miriam Russo and Donna Corey, Gottex; Byron Lars and Maria Elena, Byron Lars/Wheaton International; Bette-Ann Gwathmey, Ralph Lauren; Jun Kanai and Nancy Knox, Issey Miyake; Yasuko Suita and Haruko Enomoto, Hanae Mori; Todd Oldham, Tony Longoria, and Michael Kearney, Todd Oldham; Amelia Gonzalez and Alex Melendez, Onward Kashiyama/Jean Paul Gaultier; Michelle Stein and Lisa Salisbury, Rifat Ozbek/Moda & Company; Oscar de la Renta and Frankie Crocker, Oscar de la Renta; Connie Uzzo, Yves Saint Laurent; Ronaldus Shamask; Bruce Hoeksema and Cristina Bonolis, Valentino; Gianni Versace and Patrizia Cucco, Gianni Versace.

We are grateful for the cooperation of Mme F. Kartouby, Agence Photographique de la Reunion des Musées Nationaux; Eric de Brun, Art Resource; Horst and Richard Tardiff, Horst P. Horst; Marie McFeely, National Gallery of Ireland, and the staff of the Photograph and Slide Library, The Metropolitan Museum of Art.

We are both emboldened and abetted in every way by the superb colleagues and good friends we enjoy in The Costume Institute: Meredith Burns, Helen Chung, Deirdre Donohue, Michael Downer, Gisele Ferrari, Debbie Juchem, Rita Kauneckas, Joell Kunath, Jennifer Loveman, Kathleen Mahieu, Chris Paulocik, Dennita Sewell, and Melinda Watt. We are deeply indebted to every one of these colleagues.

Of a slightly wider world, we are grateful for others in The Metropolitan Museum of Art who have encouraged, nourished, and contributed to this enterprise: Jerri Dodds, Phylis Fogelson, Harold Holzer, Dan Kershaw, Sue Koch, Kent Lydecker, Richard R. Morsches, Chris Noey, Olga Raggio, Jennifer Russell, Linda M. Sylling, Mahrukh Tarapor, H. Barbara Weinberg, and Zack Zanolli. Philippe de Montebello believes that twains shall meet in The Metropolitan Museum of Art, if nowhere else; he is ever our gentle guide.

From the Museum's Editorial Department, John P. O'Neill, Barbara Burn, Barbara Cavaliere, Bruce Campbell, Matthew Pimm, Rob Weisberg, and Peter Antony have made this book a smooth crossing to a far aspiration; we are grateful for their forbearance and fortitude.

Many quote Rudyard Kipling's phrase that "East is East, and West is West, and never the twain shall meet." Let us not forget that he finishes his thought: "But there is neither East nor West, Border, nor Breed, nor Birth, / When two strong men stand face to face, though they come from the ends of the earth!" Fashion has always sought the ends of the earth.

RM & HK